110 Fun Facts
About God's Creation

Other Books in Liguori's "Fun Facts" Series

English
115 Saintly Fun Facts
130 Fun Facts From God's Wonder-Filled World
131 FUN-damental Facts for Catholic Kids
150 Fun Facts Found in the Bible
365 Fun Facts for Catholic Kids

Spanish
115 anécdotas en la vida de los santos
150 curiosades de la Biblia

Bean,

Love
Nana

110 Fun Facts About God's Creation

Is It Animal, Vegetable, or Mineral?

Bernadette McCarver Snyder

Liguori
LIGUORI, MISSOURI

Dedication

I dedicate this book to kids of all ages—
and to all the ladies in my prayer/share group
and to all the gab-n-gallivant WACYs
and to all who like to explore and discover all the things
God created and put into this world for us to enjoy,
to treasure—and to protect!

Imprimi Potest:
Thomas D. Picton, C.Ss.R.
Provincial, Denver Province
The Redemptorists

Published by Liguori Publications
Liguori, Missouri
To order, call 800-325-9521
www.liguori.org

Library of Congress Cataloging-in-Publication Data

Snyder, Bernadette McCarver.
   110 fun facts about God's creation : is it animal, vegetable, or mineral? / Bernadette McCarver Snyder.—1st ed.
      p. cm.
   ISBN 978-0-7648-1861-5
   1. Creation—Miscellanea—Juvenile literature. I. Title.
   BT695.S6 2010
   242'.62—dc22

                                                          2009044795

Liguori Publications, a nonprofit corporation, is an apostolate of the Redemptorists. To learn more about the Redemptorists, visit Redemptorists.com.

Printed in the United States of America
14 13 12 11 10   5 4 3 2 1
First edition

Table of Contents

Vegetable

Mineral

Extra! Extra! Bonus Section Just For Fun

Introduction

Once upon a time, long, long ago, someone, somewhere, decided that all things on the earth could fit into one of three different groups—animals, vegetables, or minerals.

Now this must have taken a lot of thinking, because it meant that the group known as *animals* would include large, small, big, or tall animals PLUS birds, fish, and even people! To remember this, you might think up a poem like

> Lions, tigers, and bears,
> Fish and fowl and birds of blue,
> Furred or feathered, fins or feet,
> And guess what?—people too!

Then when you come to the group known as *vegetables*, you will find this does not include just squash and carrots. It also includes fruit, flowers, and plants. So you might think

> Green broccoli, spinach, and asparagus,
> Pink peaches, purple pansies, and a white daisy,
> Dandelions, houseplants, and trees too.
> This mix–in–one group sure sounds crazy!

Now the last class—*minerals*—must include everything other than animals and vegetables! For instance, it includes jewels and rocks with strange names such as igneous, sedimentary, and metamorphic! So you might think of

> Diamonds, rubies, and pearls,
> Salt and sulfur, rock and rocket,
> Marble statues and airplane parts,
> Or a chunk of gravel in your pocket.

Dive into this book and discover all the treasures of God's creation.

Animals

(From Aardvark to Zebra—Plus People!)

Elephants and eagles,
Turtles and tarantulas,
Snips and snails and puppy dog tales.

How Is an Aardvark Like a Hot Rod Automobile?

Did you know that people who like to work on automobiles sometimes make a car out of spare parts from other cars? They use a hood from one car and maybe doors, bumpers, or seats from other cars. They sometimes even redo the motor to make it go really fast, and then they call this spare-parts car a hot rod.

Well, that's the kind of an animal an aardvark is. It looks like God made it out of spare parts! It has a piglike snout of a nose, ears like a donkey, and a thick tail like a kangaroo! And guess what it likes to eat? It likes to tear into termite nests and slurp up the tiny termites with its long thin tongue. But God did NOT put a souped-up motor in it so it's not EXACTLY like a hot rod.

Did you ever make anything out of spare parts? Maybe you did. When you dressed today, did you put together some spare parts to wear—shoes, socks, shirt, pants, sweater, or jacket?

Did you ever help out in the kitchen and put together some spare parts—eggs, milk, sugar, flour—to make a cake or pancakes?

Now imagine you could make a new animal out of spare parts as God did. What would you use—head of a dog, trunk from an elephant, body of a camel, and puffy tail from a rabbit? What would you call it? A delecarab? A gantelbit? It wouldn't be easy to find a name, would it? Maybe that's why God's spare-parts animal is called an aardvark!

Why Would a Frog Need a Parachute?

Have you ever played with or touched the kind of frog that lives by a pond or lake or maybe in your own backyard? Did you know there's another kind of frog, an Asian tree frog, that lives in trees and flies the way people can fly with a parachute? Now how can a frog do that? Well, God made this frog with very long toes, and in between each toe God put a fold of skin like the webs on a duck's feet. When this frog wants to move to a different tree, it leaps into the air, and its webbed feet fill with air as a parachute does—and it floats down to the tree next door!

God did not give YOU webbed feet, because he knew those toes would not fit into your favorite shoes. God knew the tree frog needed webbed feet but YOU don't. You need the kind of feet you have so you can walk, jump, run, or maybe ride a bike or skateboard. But just for today, why don't you pretend to be a tree frog, flying in the air, looking down at the jungle? Imagine you see a bird, a snake, a rock, a monkey, and lots of leaves and flowers. It's fun to pretend. Aren't you glad God gave you an imagination instead of parachute toes?

Do Fish Ever Go to School?

Well, yes, fish DO go to school! They don't carry schoolbooks or sit at a desk or use a computer the way you might do. But when you see a group of them swimming along together, this is known as a school" of fish. They often travel together because it's safer—the same way it's safer for a group of children to walk to school together instead of alone. One of the fish God made is called the PENCIL fish. Wouldn't it be funny to see a school of pencils swimming together? Why don't you get out your pencil—or pen or computer—today, and make a list of all the fish God made? See how many you can find.

You may be surprised to learn how MANY kinds of fish God made—and each so different! Tiny goldfish, huge whales, kissing fish, butterfly fish, clown fish. Just like people—they're all different, all interesting, all made by God!

Beep! Beep! Did You Ever Watch a Roadrunner Cartoon?

In the cartoons, this funny-looking bird goes racing down the road, going "Beep! Beep!"—and getting into all kinds of trouble. Well, this is all make-believe, but God DID make a REAL bird called the roadrunner. And it acts a lot like the one in the cartoon. The roadrunner lives in the desert, so it goes speeding down a road or across the desert and then it will suddenly zoom to the right or veer to the left or just stop for a second and then race ahead again—like some of the cars in movie chase scenes!

Now you've probably seen a lot of birds that fly around the sky or quietly hop around your yard, so how can the roadrunner run so fast and then make such quick stops and turns? Why? Because God gave it a long black tail that it can use like a BRAKE when it wants to stop or like a RUDDER when it makes a sudden turn.

Although the roadrunner seems to always be running, it does stop to build a nest for its bird family. But where do you think it puts the nest? Well, it lives in the desert where there are a lot of cactus plants growing but not many trees, so the roadrunner makes a saucer-shaped nest and puts it in a cactus! If you've ever touched a cactus, you know it has sharp prickly thorns all over it, so it does not seem like the friendliest spot to build a home. But the roadrunner makes do with whatever is available in the place where God put it. And maybe the roadrunner is smart too, because the thorny cactus can protect the nest more than a tree could!

The next time you or your family must make do—with a cheaper car or vacation—or do WITHOUT something you really want but don't NEED, be smart like the roadrunner and be grateful for all the things you already HAVE.

Beep! Beep!

5

Can You Guess What These Three Animals Have in Common— Monkeys, Hogs, and Weasels?

Monkeys, hogs, and weasels have NAMES that can also be used as verbs—action words. Think about that the next time you hear someone say, "Don't MONKEY around." (They mean you should hurry up because you are taking too much time to clean your room or do a chore or help someone who needs your help.)

Or someone might tell you, "Don't HOG the TV" or "Don't WEASEL out of doing your homework."

Of course, you would never do any of those three things, would you?

20

6

Do You Think Saint Francis Ever Tried to Talk to the Birds?

When you hear a bird singing, do you ever try to tweet or whistle to see if you can get the bird to talk back to you? Maybe Saint Francis did that too, because every time you see a statue or picture of him there is a bird perched on his shoulder or sitting at his feet.

Even if Saint Francis never talked to the birds, he loved all birds and animals—and cared for them and protected them. But Saint Francis lived in Italy in a small town called Assisi, and he didn't travel far away, so he probably never got to see all the different kinds of birds YOU can see. If you go to a zoo or an animal park, you might see colorful tropical birds such as the toucan or the bird of paradise. You might see an eagle or a falcon or a peacock. But you probably wouldn't have to go very far to see lots of different birds in your own neighborhood. You could care for and protect the birds as Saint Francis did if you could put a bird feeder or a birdbath in your yard. But you would have to remember to put out food and/or water every day so the birds won't be disappointed when they stop by your "restaurant" to get a bite to eat or a drink of water or even to take a splish-splashy bath! Wouldn't that be fun to watch!

7

Why Would a River Horse Yawn?

The name HIPPOPOTAMUS really means river horse, and hippos DO spend most of its time in a river—or in a pond or a lake or a zoo where you might see one. During the day, the huge hippo likes to float in the water with only its ears and the top of its head to be seen. But at night, it comes out to graze on grasses and other land plants. And if you ever see one yawn, it's not because the hippo is bored or sleepy but because it is showing its big teeth to warn off anything that is threatening it—the same way a dog sometimes growls and shows its teeth. Do you ever yawn when you get bored or sleepy? The next time you yawn, use that as a trigger to remind you of how God made so many nonboring, interesting things in the world for you to discover. Try to choose which one is your favorite thing that God made, and say a quick little prayer to tell God thanks and explain to God why it is your favorite.

8

Which Would You Nominate to Be the World's Worst Bug or Best Bug?

You might have to think a bit about which you think is the worst or best bug, because there are maybe hundreds of different kinds of creepy, crawly bugs in or on God's earth. But here's an idea: you could nominate the litterbug as being the worst kind of bug!

Of course, a litterbug is not a real bug—it's the name for someone who is careless and/or lazy and just tosses out candy wrappers, banana peels, or any kind of trash in the city, on the roadside, or at any public area. By thoughtlessly littering, this person can make any area ugly when it could be and should be clean and beautiful. That's BAD.

Now what about the best bug? Why not choose the bookworm? Again, this is not a real worm but someone who loves to read books and learn new things. Now that's a way to worm yourself into an intelligent and interesting life! That's GOOD.

Which one are you—a litterbug or a bookworm, a worst or best? Or do you think maybe God made you just a little bit of each? Think about it.

9

Did You Ever Hear of Florence Nightingale, Amelia Earhart, Mother Teresa, or Louise de Marillac?

You know the animal category includes people too, and there are many men and women who did something unusual or made a difference in God's world—but here are just four you might like to hear about.

Florence Nightingale organized a group of nurses to care for wounded British soldiers in the Crimean War. After that, she founded the Nightingale School and Home for nurse training and became known as the founder of modern nursing.

Amelia Earhart was an aviator who became the first woman to fly solo across the Atlantic Ocean.

Mother Teresa was a quiet nun who cared for dying people in India and won the Nobel Peace Prize.

And Saint Louise de Marillac was a widow who opened soup kitchens, hospitals, and schools throughout France and founded an order of nuns known as the Daughters of Charity, who have continued her work across the world. Although she had poor health and a very busy schedule, Louise was known always to be pleasant and cheerful.

Would you like to do something unusual and/or make a difference in God's world? You wouldn't have to do something dramatic such as fly solo across the Atlantic Ocean or win a Nobel prize. But you COULD try to help anyone you can and try to be pleasant and cheerful even when you have some hard work to do. And you can start to think today of what you would like to do some day in the future—maybe found some new kind of business or charity, set some kind of record, become a Catholic nun or priest? Pray for God to lead you in the way he wants you to go and try to follow the example of some of the men and women God made to make a difference.

Did You Know Ducks Dabble— and Also Babysit?

God made two main groups of ducks—dabblers and divers.

The diving ducks dive completely under water to hunt for food, but most of them live out at sea. The dabblers put most of their body into the water and kick their webbed feet backward to go forward! Instead of deep diving, they feed at the surface of the water, so you can often see them floating around or sometimes walking around ponds or lakes.

And sometime you might even see some of them baby-sitting! Ducks and geese often run nursery schools. A few adults will babysit the children of other birds. Some of the duck schools may have as many as one hundred little ducklings.

One day you might even see a line of traffic stopped on a street near a pond— waiting for geese or ducks to cross. Usually one adult will watch for a break in traffic, then start across, and all the little ducklings will group together and follow with a few adults bringing up the rear to watch for stragglers. And all the in-a-hurry cars just have to stop and wait for the ducky-daddles-crossing.

If God had made you like a duck, would you rather be a dabbler or a diver—or maybe even a babysitter?

Did You Ever See a Bug With Bioluminescence?

You might not know it—but you probably HAVE seen a bug with bioluminescence! This is just a fancy word for the special biochemical God put into a LIGHTNING BUG. That's what makes it possible for a firefly to turn on its flashlight in a dark night.

Do you think God made such fun bugs so that you can go out in your backyard on a summer night and enjoy watching the lightning bugs blink and flash their lights in the dark, possibly sending signals to other fireflies?

Why don't you get a flashlight and go out in your backyard some night and pretend God made you a firefly! Run around the yard flashing signals to some imaginary secret super spy with your flashlight and quietly saying a little prayer of thanks that the REAL God made such fun bugs. If you do that, maybe the lightning bugs will start watching YOU instead of you watching them!

Do You Know How Many Birds There Are in the World?

There are about one hundred MILLION birds in the world! Are you surprised to hear that? And did you know it takes about 25,000 feathers to cover one swan and about 950 feathers to cover a tiny little ruby-throated hummingbird? And did you know that a hummingbird has fourteen tiny bones just in its neck—which is twice as many bones as there are in a tall giraffe's neck?

And here's another fun fact— about three million of those birds in the world are chickens! Those chickens lay lots of eggs for your breakfast, but there is also one BIG bird named an ostrich that lays very BIG eggs. So if you wanted to make scrambled eggs for a big family, you would need only ONE ostrich egg, because one ostrich egg equals EIGHTEEN chicken eggs!

And here's another fun fact. Some birds have double names like the riroriro (a New Zealand warbler), the zoozoo (a ringdove), and the see-see (a West Asian sand partridge).

The next time you go to Mass or are saying your prayers at bedtime, tell God you are very-very glad-glad he made so many fun-fun things in nature for you to discover and then tell God thank you–thank you.

Have You Ever Been As Busy As a Bee?

According to a reputable source, one bee must make 4,200 trips to flowers to make one tablespoon of honey! The person who counted those 4,200 trips must have been as busy as a bee too! If YOU want to be as busy as a bee, why don't you COUNT all the blessings God has given you? The first one you might count is the fact that you would NOT have to make 4,200 trips to the grocery to get a whole JAR of honey!

14

Did You Ever Have Bamboo for Breakfast?

Bamboo for breakfast would be a BAD boondoggle for YOU—because bamboo has sharp splinters in it. But panda bears eat bamboo for breakfast, lunch, and dinner! That's why God made the panda's throat with a tough lining but made YOUR throat with a softer lining—just right for pancakes or pizza for breakfast.

AND to help the panda start the day with bamboo, God gave the bear a sixth finger! This finger is a bit like a thumb, and it grows out of the panda bear's WRIST. This makes it easy for the panda to hold the bamboo stalk while it strips off the coarse outside and then eats the inside. And the panda needs all that help because it strips and eats about 600 bamboo stems every day!

You might never see a giant panda bear because it lives in the misty mountain forests of China, but you might see some of the other kinds of bears God made if you visit a zoo—the black bear, the brown bear, the grizzly bear, and the polar bear.

Actually, a zoo would be the beary best place to see any kind of bear because none of them are very friendly to people—except the teddy bear!

15

What Do You Know About the Ibex, Ibis, or Iguana?

If you looked up the ibex, the ibis, and the iguana in a dictionary, you would find they are all very different—so can you guess what these three have in common?

The ibex is a wild goat with horns that curve backward. You might find one on the highest, coldest mountain tops.

The ibis is a wading bird with a long bill that curves downward. Some have bright scarlet red feathers, and you might find one in warm tropical lagoons.

The iguana is a pretty ugly looking lizard that doesn't have horns or a bill but can grow to about six feet long, so you might find one in a tropical tree OR in a comfy cage, eating insects and leaves, at a pet store!

The fun fact about these three is that they have I-appeal. They are probably the only animals with names that start with the letter I!

But wait! Remember that there are human "animals" too, and some of them have names that start with the letter I. In fact, there are also some saints whose names have I-appeal. They include Saints Isidore, Ida, Idesbald, Imbert, Ingleby, Irenaeus, and Ixida. Do you have any friends with those saint names? Probably not, but you may have a friend named Isabel or Ignatius—those are saints' names too. Try to think of all the people you know who have names with I-appeal, and then tell God thanks for all the animals and all the saints and all the friends who have I-nteresting names.

16

Did You Ever See a Statue of a Horse?

In a park, you might see all kinds of statues, and some of them might be a statue of a famous man riding a horse, so you know the statue was made to honor the man, not the horse. And if the famous man was a famous soldier, there is a legend about the way the horse is standing. For example, if the horse has both front legs in the air, the man riding it died in battle. If the horse has only one front leg in the air, the soldier died because of wounds he received in battle. And if the horse has all four legs on the ground, the lucky man survived the war and maybe even became more famous after the war, like Ulysses Grant, who became president of the United States.

Did you ever ride a horse or think about all the ways horses help people? Some horses have to be very brave to ride into battle with the sound of gunfire all around them. Some have to get used to the noise of traffic because they are the horses police ride to patrol busy city streets. Some work hard on farms to pull heavy loads, and some live at a livery stable where people can come and ride them just for the joy of riding. And some very special horses are trained to be racehorses and have to learn to run very fast—so fast that they sometimes wear out a new set of horseshoes in ONE race.

How fast do you wear out a new set of shoes? Aren't you glad they are made of something softer than horseshoes? Tell God thanks today for shoes and horseshoes and horses and heroes who rode horses.

Do You Know What a Leveret or a Cygnet Is?

You probably know that a young horse is a colt, a young cow is a calf, a young goat is a kid, a young dog is a puppy, and a young cat is a kitten, but did you know that a young hare (or rabbit) is a leveret, and a young swan is a cygnet? And guess what they call a young kangaroo? They call it a joey.

Do you know anyone called Joey? Do you have a friend, uncle, cousin, or neighbor named Joseph? People often use Joey as a nickname for Joseph—unless they're talking about Saint Joseph! People don't usually give nicknames to saints—but maybe when Saint Joseph was young, his mother might have called him Joey. Who knows?

Ask your mother if she had a special name for YOU when you were little—a name like Snookums, Cutesywootsie, Honeylamb, or Sugarbaby? If she did, you might like it— or you might want to ask her NEVER to tell it to any of your friends.

You Ought-Er See This Otter!

The animal named an otter is a lot like kids. It likes to wander around and explore. It romps along riverbanks or the seashore, jumping in and out of the water, playing as a kid would at a swimming pool. It likes to roam over land looking for new fishing spots and loves to play by sliding down a bank of snow or mud. Does that sound like anyone you know?

The sea otter knows how to use "tools" too—which is very unusual for an animal. Sometimes the otter gathers some seaweed and uses it like rope to tie together the family so that no one will float away in a strong current. And you'll never guess what an otter does at suppertime. It floats on its back, balances a rock on its tummy, grabs a clam, smashes it on the rock to break the shell, and has a clam dinner.

Playing along a river or sliding down a bank of mud sounds like fun, but aren't you glad God made you so you can eat dinner at a table with a napkin on your lap instead of a rock on your tummy?

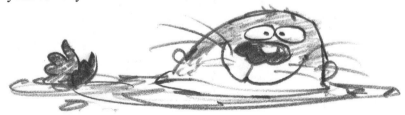

19

God Made So Many Useful Parts of Your Body Like Ears and Eyes, Feet and Hands—But Do You Know What Your Right Hand Can Do That Your Left Hand Can't?

Only your right hand can touch your left elbow! Of course, only your left hand can touch your right elbow—so it all works out OK.

Did you ever try to elbow your way through a crowd or to the front of a line? That's really not a great thing to do. It's rude, Dude!

Did you ever use "elbow grease" to work hard and get a hard job done? That really is a great thing to do. It's gude, Dude!

Aren't you glad God gave you elbows so you can reach high places, wave to a friend, or tip your baseball cap after you've played a great game? How many other times can you remember when you NEEDED an elbow?

Do Santa's Reindeer Wear Snowshoes?

You've heard lots of stories about Santa and his reindeer, but did you know that God gave real reindeer a kind of snowshoe feet? He did! The reindeer has broad hooves on its feet to make it easier for it to walk in deep snow—and, as you probably know, reindeer live where the snow is REALLY deep.

The reindeer also uses its hooves as a snow scraper. Did you ever see someone using a scraper to get snow off a car's windshield? In the same way, the reindeer uses a hoof to carefully scrape snow away from the ground so it can nibble the nice green grass that grows beneath the snow.

And did you know that another name for reindeer is caribou? And did you know Eskimos like to drink reindeer milk? And did you know that lots of reindeer take a trip twice a year? They do!

They sometimes travel as far as 600 miles, following trails that the reindeer families have used for hundreds of years. There are two places they like to visit. Half the year, they live on the tundra, which is a treeless plain, and, the other half, they live in forests where lots of Christmas trees grow.

Do you like to travel? Why don't you pretend today that you are traveling to the tundra, wearing snowshoes to visit the snowshoe reindeer, and having cookies with a glass of reindeer milk?

21

Do Birds Ever Wear Camouflage?

God is full of surprises, so he made some birds that wear "camouflage." Many young birds look different from their parents—until they grow up. The herring gull hatches with a camouflage coating of fluffy, gray down spotted with black. When it gets its "flight feathers" it becomes dark brown. It keeps molting (losing feathers) until it is wearing the crisp gray and white "uniform" of an adult gull.

Some birds have very bright feathers in the spring but lose them and become gray or brown by fall. The bird called a ptarmigan has white feathers in the winter to match the snow-covered areas where it lives, but by summer it has molted and has become a mottled (mixed) brown that will blend in with the summer ground and rocks.

So birds keep changing clothes for different reasons in different seasons, just as you change from warm winter woolies into summertime coolies.

Do you ever like to wear camouflage—to wear clothes made from the kind of camouflage-colored material soldiers wear? Or do you like to dress up and camouflage yourself with a cape or a hat or a mustache so you can pretend to be a superhero or a movie star? Did you know that some of the saints were superheroes and had adventurous lives? Why don't you ask someone to tell you a hero-saint story, and then you could pretend to be a saint instead of a movie star?

Did You Know Buckingham Palace Has More Than 600 Rooms?

If you think it takes a lot of time to clean your room, how would you like to clean 600 rooms? But that's just one of the many fun facts about this palace and the people who have lived there.

Did you know that there have been six kings of England named George—and the first King George of England could not speak English! If he wanted someone to clean his room, he couldn't even tell them where to start.

Actually it wasn't his fault. George I was a German who inherited the British throne, so he probably wondered why all those British people couldn't speak German.

Would you like to learn a foreign language? Many people around the world today can speak English as a second language to their native language, but very few Americans can speak anything other than English. It might be fun for you to learn Spanish or French or whatever. Then when you were told to clean your room, you could reply in something other than English!

You could also learn how to pray in different languages—which would be OK because God speaks ALL languages and hears ALL prayers.

23

Do You Know the Difference Between Cassocks and Cossacks?

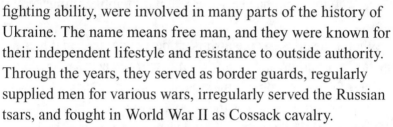

The people known as Cossacks, famed for their horsemanship and fighting ability, were involved in many parts of the history of Ukraine. The name means free man, and they were known for their independent lifestyle and resistance to outside authority. Through the years, they served as border guards, regularly supplied men for various wars, irregularly served the Russian tsars, and fought in World War II as Cossack cavalry.

Today families of those early Cossacks have retained their skills in horsemanship and sometimes wear the traditional outfit of wide trousers tucked into boots, bright sashes, and red silk–topped caps. Some have formed a popular traveling show that presents folk dancing and amazing examples of their unique horsemanship. And you probably won't be surprised to hear that there is also a Cossacks computer game.

But a cassock is something very different. It's the simple ankle-length black vestment worn by Catholic priests and sometimes by deacons, altar boys and girls, or possibly choir members. Those cassocks have been around a long time in history too. You can see pictures of priests all over the world, in the past and the present, wearing those long, black cassocks.

Just changing the letter A to an O makes a huge difference. This is an example of how important it is always to watch your language! If you don't, you might accidentally change a priest in a cassock into a fighting Cossack! Someone may tell you to watch your P's and Q's, but you better also watch your A's and O's.

Did You Ever See a Bird That Seems to Be Walking on Water?

Birds like water, so you've probably seen them wading, but did you know there are some birds that "walk" on top of the water? One of them is called a coot. It's a dark gray, ducklike bird that lives in wetlands and has very big feet with flaplike things along its toes.

When it decides to take a walk, it beats its wings and feet very fast to build up speed, and then it scurries across the top of the water, like a speedboat, making sprays and splashes all over.

Another water walker is the jaçana, which has the nickname of "lily-trotter." It can walk over a "carpet" of lily pads and floating plants without ever sinking in. That's because, like the coot, it has very long toes and toenails, which help it spread its weight and keep its balance.

You've probably heard the Bible story about the time Jesus walked on water, but I bet you were surprised to hear about water-walking birds.

Do you like to wade in water or swim? In the summertime, do you like to run through the sprinkler? The next time you do that, pretend you are a bird, and walk calmly across the grass the way the jaçana walks across the lily pads or race around spraying and splashing like the coot. What a hoot!

Did You Ever Feel As Sick As a Dog?

There are a lot of "old sayings" about animals: "You're as strong as an ox; you're as wise as an owl; you're as cunning as a fox." Did you ever hear any of those funny sayings? It would be a good idea to be strong, wise, and maybe cunning, but why would somebody think being sick would be like a dog?

You've probably seen lots of healthy, happy dogs, but have you ever seen an ox, an owl, or a fox? God made them all very different but gave them each a special "talent" such as being strong or wise or cunning. Do you think God gave YOU a special talent? Well, he did.

Maybe God gave you a voice to sing or athletic ability to play sports or a good mind to solve problems or a smiling face and good humor that makes everybody happy to be with you. Think about it. What do you think is your special talent? Could it be that you are "as straight as an arrow," "as sharp as a tack," "as neat as a pin," or "as good as gold"?

26

How Is a Cassowary Like a Watermelon?

A cassowary is a strange kind of bird. It's short-legged and stout-bodied, and its wing feathers look more like hair than feathers. But the strangest thing of all is that the cassowary wears a helmet! This definitely sets it apart from other birds. The bony helmet is flattened like a blade and perched on the forehead. It may look funny, but it seems to have a good purpose. It seems to protect the big bird as it makes its way through thick, thorny bushes or weedy undergrowth.

But if you think that helmet is strange, did you know that many, many years ago some Greek and Roman soldiers used dried-out watermelons for helmets?

Why don't you cut a watermelon in half and get someone to help you hollow it out and eat all the juicy good fruit inside. Then you can put the watermelon half somewhere safe where it won't rot and wait for it to dry out.

While you're waiting, you can think about how God made two such different things as watermelons and cassowaries. Then you can put the dried watermelon on your head and decide if you think it would make a good helmet. But if you do that, you know people might laugh and call you a strange bird!

27

Do You Know a Secret About Walt Disney, Thomas Edison, and Bugs Bunny?

Walt Disney, who created Disneyland and Mickey Mouse, was afraid of mice! Thomas Edison, who invented the light bulb, was afraid of the dark. And Mel Blanc, the man who was the voice of Bugs Bunny, was allergic to carrots—so he was afraid to crunch on them as Bugs did, knowing it would make him sick!

They all had something to fear. Actually, almost everyone is afraid of some little things—and maybe a big thing, too—but they don't talk about it very much. They'd rather keep it secret. But it might help if they DID talk about it to a friend.

Are you afraid of anything? There are some things you SHOULD be afraid of—crossing the street without looking both ways, riding in a car without wearing a seatbelt, or eating ice cream so fast you get brain freeze. But ALWAYS being afraid can give you brain freeze too.

If you're afraid of something like the dark or a mouse or a carrot, just try to be brave, and maybe soon you'll get over it. But when something big comes along that you should be afraid of, try to talk to someone about it and get help, then grit your teeth and quietly and secretly ask God to hold your hand.

28

How Does an "Achoo" Lead to a "God Bless You"?

When you have a cold or it's allergy time and pollen or dust gets into your nose, the nose KNOWS something is there that should NOT be, and it sends a message to your brain to get rid of it. That's when your throat closes, air pressure builds up in your lungs, and kaboom—you sneeze. During a good sneeze, air flies out of your lungs at about one hundred miles an hour! Did you know your sneezes can travel faster than a car going over the speed limit?

Back before medicines such as antibiotics had been discovered, even simple colds or the flu could develop into serious infections. So when you sneezed, people would wish you a safe recovery. Some would say to you, "Gesundheit," which is German for "good health."

Others would say "God bless you" to let you know they cared about you and wanted you to get well. And it became a tradition, so people still say that today.

Although people seem to be the animals that suffer most from colds and allergies, dogs, cats, and some other animals can have allergies too. But if you said "Gesundheit" to your pets, they would probably think you were just sneezing again!

Aren't you glad doctors and scientists have discovered so many ways to treat sickness today? When someone sneezes, it's good to say a prayer for the sneezer but also a reminder to say a prayer of thanks for doctors, scientists, and all the people who care enough to say, "God bless you."

29

What Do You Think Is the Smallest— or the Largest—Bug That God Made?

Bugs come in all sizes. There are tiny wasps that are called "fairy flies" that are only one hundredth of an inch long. That's so tiny, you might need a magnifying glass to get a good look at it. There are also giant stick insects that are twelve inches long (that's as long as a foot). And the Goliath beetles really are gigantic! One of those beetles could weigh as much as a hamster! They look pretty scary, but they are harmless. Some children in the rainforests of Africa even keep them as pets! Did

you ever have a hamster as a pet? If you could choose any kind of pet to own, would you choose a fairy fly, a stick insect, or a beetle? Probably not—but it IS interesting to learn about all the kinds of buggy, creepy, or crawly things God made. What pet WOULD you choose—a pony, a polar bear, a possum, a panda, or maybe a puppy or a kitten?

30

Did You Ever Hear the Song About Davy, Davy Crockett—King of the Wild Frontier?

Davy Crockett lived a long time ago and was a "folk hero" who was so interesting that Disney later made a TV series about him, and everyone was singing the theme song about "Davy, Davy Crockett." He was a frontiersman, a soldier, and a politician. He grew up in the woods and learned survival skills and was a great hunter and fisherman, but then he got interested in politics, got himself elected to Congress, and went from the wild frontier to Washington. He was a colorful figure with his coonskin hat, backwoods clothes, and tall tales. He would say things like "I'm half-horse and half-alligator, with a little touch of the snapping turtle. I have got the roughest horse, the prettiest sister, and the ugliest dog in the district."

Did you ever meet someone who was a great hunter or an elected congressman or a "folk hero" with tall tales to tell?

In the Bible, Jesus met ALL kinds of people—like Zacharias, who climbed a tree to get Jesus' attention, and the man who was a leper but was healed by Jesus. People followed Jesus wherever he went so they could hear his message of "Good News." At that time, some people probably thought of Jesus as a folk hero, because they didn't know yet, as we do, that he is our Savior.

Do you like to hear Bible stories about the things Jesus did when he was on earth? Why don't you ask someone to read you a bedtime story from the Bible tonight?

31

Did You Ever See a Toy Called Mr. Potato Head?

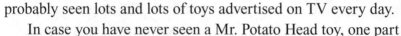

Did you know Mr. Potato Head was the FIRST toy ever to be advertised on television? That was a looong time ago—before you were born! Today you have probably seen lots and lots of toys advertised on TV every day.

In case you have never seen a Mr. Potato Head toy, one part looks just like a big potato. Then there's a collection of different kinds of face parts—such as eyes, ears, and nose—so you can have fun making a Mr. Potato face and then start over and over, each time giving him a different funny "face."

The next time you're sitting in church or walking down a mall, look around at all the different faces of people you see. Notice how each person has a big or little nose, blue or brown eyes, a round face or a long one. Isn't it amazing how God only has a few "face parts" to work with, and yet God makes so many people look so different. Each person has a face that may be similar to someone else's face, but none of them are exactly the same. Even twins have faces that are just a bit different in some way.

God was so careful when he made our world. God made flowers of all kinds and colors, trees and bushes with different kinds of leaves, and lots of different animals, birds, and fish. Wouldn't the world be boring if God hadn't made so many "differences" for you to enjoy? Start looking around every day, noticing and thanking God for so many "differences."

Did You Ever Have Lunch With a Grasshopper?

If you did—or if you ever do—have lunch with a grasshopper, you might notice that when a grasshopper chews, it moves its jaws back and forth instead of up and down the way you do. When it's not eating, the grasshopper does what you might expect—it hops through grass! And it is NOT easy to catch. God gave the grasshopper special legs that can help it hop high and leap two or three or four times the length of its body! Do you think you could leap that high? You can probably hop and leap high, but you are a lot "longer" than a grasshopper, so you would have to leap a lot higher. If God had given you legs like a grasshopper, you might look strange, but you could probably leap right over your house!

Aren't you glad God gave you the kind of legs you need to hop into the kitchen and bite into a pizza or hot dog with your "choppers"? Tell God thanks for fun foods—and for choppers and hoppers!

33

How Is an Emu Like a Kangaroo?

An emu and a kangaroo DO have names that rhyme, but there's another fun fact about them. Strange as it may seem, neither of them can walk backward!

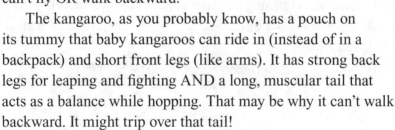

That must mean that if they want to go back where they came from, they would have to turn around and walk forward to go backward!

In case you don't know, the emu is a large, dark-plumed Australian bird that has powerful legs and is a strong runner—but it can't fly OR walk backward.

The kangaroo, as you probably know, has a pouch on its tummy that baby kangaroos can ride in (instead of in a backpack) and short front legs (like arms). It has strong back legs for leaping and fighting AND a long, muscular tail that acts as a balance while hopping. That may be why it can't walk backward. It might trip over that tail!

It's very unusual that these very different animals could be alike in any way, but you might notice that they are also a bit like your family car. Your car can go backward for a short distance, but to get back where it came from it has to turn around, so it has to go backward to go forward!

Aren't you glad you can walk backward AND forward? Take a nice walk somewhere today and look around and see what you can see that maybe you never saw before!

34

Why Doesn't a Bird Fall Off Its Perch When It Goes to Sleep?

Songbirds—like wrens and sparrows, waxwings and magpies—are known as perching birds, and their perching secret is in their toes. God made them with three toes in the front and one stronger toe that points to the rear. When the bird lands on a branch, its back toe automatically locks around the branch from below, and the other toes pull tight from the front. Those "locking toes" keep it from tumbling off even if the branch is swaying in the wind or if the bird decides to take a nap! And birds don't just perch on branches. You might see them on telephone wires, fence posts, or the very tiptop of a tall tree.

Would you like to have "locking toes" so you could sit on a branch or a telephone wire? That might be fun at first, but bird feet would not be good for chasing your best friend around the playground or swimming fast in a pool or riding a bicycle! So enjoy watching the birds, and tell God thanks for bird feet AND your own people feet.

35

Do Birds Do Anything Besides Just Fly, Perch, and Sing?

Although those three wonderful things would be enough, you may be surprised to know that God did not just make beautiful birds in many colors to decorate the sky and entertain people with their singing and flitting about. Birds also help keep down the numbers of destructive insects or other pests by eating huge quantities of mosquitoes and flies and leaf-destroying insects.

And some birds even probe a lawn with their beaks, getting out the grubs that can destroy a front yard. Yep, birds are not just beautiful. They also work to help the planet and the people who live on it. Did you know some people may look beautiful like the birds or be talented enough to sing beautiful songs  or learn to fly a plane or even walk on a high wire in a circus, but they never do any kind of work to help others? Now isn't that a shame.

Does a Zebra Ever Play Football?

Probably not—but you WILL see a zebra at most football games. As you probably know, a zebra is a wild horse that God painted with black and white—or white and black—stripes. AND football referees are called zebras because they wear shirts that have black and white stripes—so you will usually see zebras at football games!

There are always crowds at big football games, and wild zebras like to travel in crowds too, because this keeps them safer from enemies. Now if you've seen a zebra in a zoo, you might think all zebras look alike, but they don't. Each has its own special stripe pattern. God made them striped this way for protection. The white looks like light and the black like shadow, and this makes them hard to spot when they are in tall grasses. To make it even safer, in a group, they face in different directions to make a zigzag pattern! Isn't that smart?

If an enemy DOES spot them, the zebras scatter and run in different directions so the zigzagging will confuse the enemy!

This gave some people a good idea during World War II. They painted merchant ships with zebra stripes so they would be harder to spot by enemy submarines!

Do you ever wear a striped shirt? Do you like to run fast? Do you sometimes try to hide from someone the way zebras hide in tall grasses? Aren't you surprised to learn that zebras have something in common with football referees, merchant ships—and YOU?

Vegetables
(Plants, Both Eatable and Not!)

Potatoes and tomatoes
(for fries and BLTs),
Daisies and dandelions,
Tall trees and tiny seeds.

Did You Ever Eat a Root, a Stem, or a Leaf?

You probably have eaten some roots, stems, and leaves, because that's what some vegetables are! And if they're cooked correctly, they can all be delicious. Yes, really delicious.

For example, did you ever have sweet potatoes cooked with marshmallows on top or put your fork into a slice of sweet potato pie for dessert? Did you know sweet potatoes and carrots are actually ROOTS of plants?

If you ever ate asparagus—maybe in vegetable soup—you might like to know that asparagus is really a plant STEM.

Cabbage (used to make slaw) and lettuce and spinach (used to make salads) are really plant LEAVES.

Some others that fit into the vegetable category—like tomatoes, peppers, and even nuts—are technically fruits. And other fruits include apples and peaches that grow on trees and peas and beans that grow on vines or bushes. Did you know that?

What is your favorite vegetable that you are happy to see on your plate? What is your best friend's favorite vegetable? The next time you eat lunch together, try to figure out together whether you're eating a root, a stem, a leaf, or technically "something else"!

And don't forget to say the Blessing Before Meals prayer before every meal—to tell God you're thankful for having so many good things to eat when many people in the world have so little.

38

Do You Know How a Plant Is Different From an Animal?

Most LIVING things on earth are either a plant or an animal. The animals seem to "get around" more than the plants. God's four-footed animals can crawl or walk around, and the two-footed ones can hop, skip, and jump or ride in a car to go from one place to another. The birds can fly all over, and the fish can swim from streams to rivers. But once plants are planted, their roots keep them from moving to another side of the garden or the street.

Yet plants are very important because ALL the animals on the earth (especially people) couldn't live without the food plants provide!

Plants can grow and spread across the yard, and their seeds can get caught by the wind or carried away by a bird and travel to another neighborhood to grow in a new place, but plants are pretty much meant to stay in their own backyard.

Some people are happy traveling from city to city for fun or for work or for adventure. Others are happy just to settle down in the city where they were born and "bloom where they were planted." Which would you rather do?

39

Do You Know the Meaning of These Words—Modicum, Miniature, or Minute?

All these words can be used to describe something that is teeny-tiny, wee, or very small. And that's just how God made many fruit, vegetable, and plant seeds—very small. Some are as small as the period you put after a sentence. Some are a bit larger, but ALL of them look kinda ugly and unimportant. This is one of God's many surprises. If planted properly, those tiny seeds can grow into beautiful flowers, fat watermelons, or tall, leafy trees. Because of those seeds, you can enjoy strawberry shortcake, corn on the cob, or a Halloween jack-o'-lantern. Those seeds are powerful! If YOU ever feel small or unimportant, remember how God made those seeds—and how God made you too. Believe in God's surprises, and know that you too are powerful. You have the power to eat good things and grow up healthy, to smile instead of frown so you can make other people happy, and to try to always act the way God would want one of his "seeds" to act!

Did You Ever Try Eating an Iceberg?

Maybe you DID eat an iceberg without knowing it! If you like salad, you might have eaten a salad that had "iceberg" lettuce in it. Now why do you think someone would name a green vegetable after a hunk of ice floating in the ocean? Do you think it was maybe because an iceberg is a piece of ice that has broken off a glacier and lettuce is something you break up into chunks before you put it in a salad? No, probably not. It might be because this particular lettuce is very crunchy and cool tasting.

Did you know God made several different TYPES of lettuce? The iceberg is a Crisphead because its leaves grow tightly together in the shape of a "head." Another lettuce is called Butterhead because its leaves form looser heads; this variety includes Bibb, Boston, Buttercrunch, and Tom Thumb lettuce. Then there's loose leaf lettuce such as romaine.

Do you like lettuce on a sandwich, a burger, or tacos? The next time you eat lettuce, pretend you are floating on an iceberg in the ocean. Look around. What do you see? If you're a Butterhead, you might just see water and wonder how you're gonna get off this iceberg. If you're a Crisphead, you might notice seagulls flying around, waves moving in different directions, and maybe even a rescue boat coming in the distance, so you can wave your arms and shout and try to thumb a ride home.

Would an Alligator Pear Be an Animal or a Vegetable?

Did you ever eat an alligator or a pear or an alligator pear? You probably have eaten a nice juicy pear but NOT an alligator. But if you like Mexican food, you may have eaten an alligator pear, because that's another name for the avocado pear that's used to make a Mexican dip for chips. Someone probably gave it the gator name because the skin on the pear is greenish, blackish, and rough and ugly like an alligator's skin. But when you peel off that skin, inside there's a pretty, yellowish-green pear that can be mixed up to make a creamy, delicious green dip called guacamole (gwaka-MO-lee). Did you ever eat that? Did it taste like an alligator or a pear to you?

On Halloween, did you ever see someone dressed in an alligator costume? They might have looked scary to you until you were surprised to find it was just a friend inside the costume!

Did you ever meet someone who seemed as grim and grouchy as a gator UNTIL you spent some time together and found out there was a very nice person hiding INside that grouchy gator outside? It's not a good idea to judge people only by the way they look on the outside. Aren't you glad God loves us all—since he knows we are his children even on days when we're acting like a mean old alligator instead of being happy enough to do a Mexican hat dance.

What Does an Ocean Liner Have to Do With an Onion?

Did you know that in ONE day, the world's farmers grow enough ONIONS to weigh 98,000 tons? That's as much as the huge ocean liner named the *Queen Elizabeth* weighs! (No, Queen Elizabeth does not weigh that much, but the ocean liner does.) Also in ONE day, the world produces more than 7,000 tons of cocoa beans—enough to make 600 million chocolate bars. The onion and the cocoa bean are very different "vegetables," but aren't you glad God made both? Which would you rather have—a hamburger with onion rings or a chocolate bar?

43

Have You Noticed That Some Vegetables Have Some Very Funny Names?

Who knows where these names came from? Why would anybody give a poor innocent vegetable a name like kohlrabi, mushroom, okra, squash, or turnip? The next time you're having vegetables for dinner, why don't you make up some funny sentences with vegetable names?

"I'm as cool as a cucumber, and my baseball team could beet your team any day!"

"I feel like a spoonful of peas, if you please."

"The next time we have a spelling bee, I'm gonna squash the competition."

"When I am telling you something important, don't turnip your nose at me."

"Oh, oh, we forgot to say the Blessing Before Meals, so lettuce pray!"

If you know some people who have interesting names, you could use the same idea to play a name game. But always be careful not to hurt someone's feelings. The vegetables probably don't care, but some of your friends might.

Would You Ever Want to Drink Something Made With Leaves?

How about frosty iced tea in the summer or cozy hot tea in the winter? Did you know tea has been a favorite drink for many, many years since the day some leaves from a tea plant accidentally blew into some boiling water—and someone tasted the brew it made—and liked it!

Today there are teacups and tea sets, teacakes and teacarts, tea parties and teahouses (where people go to drink tea from a teacup). You may have some tea bags at your house (tea leaves sealed in a bag made of filter paper and used to make tea in a hurry). You may even have a tea caddy, which is a place to keep tea leaves and is nothing like a golf caddy. You may have a teakettle that whistles when the water is hot enough to make tea. You may have a teapot where you make the tea to pour into the teacup. And all of this may sound like a "tempest in a teapot," which means making a big to-do about a small happening.

This might be a good time to take a time-out and read a book or make up a poem about leaves or say some prayers—while you sip some tea. You might like to try a flavored tea such as orange pekoe or oolong—but if you have homework to do, don't sip too long!

45

What Does a Baseball Pop Fly Have to Do With Corn?

You've probably enjoyed corn on the cob, corn pudding, or even canned corn as a dinner vegetable, but did you know that during a baseball game, when a pop fly is easily fielded, they call it a "can of corn"? Who knows where that funny name got started, but there are a lot of funny baseball names—like pop fly! There's the bullpen, knuckleball, pinch hitter, sacrifice fly, and groundout. Can you think of some others? Some baseball teams have funny names too, especially when they are Catholic-school teams. You might see a headline in the newspaper sports section announcing "St. Richard defeats Our Lady of Sorrows," "St. Joan of Arc in close battle with Holy Angels," or "Our Lady of Peace meets St. Francis of Assisi."

Baseball is known as the national sport of the United States and can be enjoyed by all ages—boys and men, girls and women—starting with Little Leagues. Do you like to watch baseball or play baseball? Do you always play by the rules?

What Do You Think About When You Hear the Word Apple?

You might think about an APPLE computer or maybe a big piece of apple pie—two very different kinds of apples. Or maybe you might think of the old saying, "An apple a day keeps the doctor away"—a reminder that you should eat an apple or some kind of fruit every day so you will be healthy and not need to see a doctor. Or you could think of Johnny Appleseed, the nickname for a man who traveled about the United States planting apple trees.

The next time you need to find a special gift for someone, maybe you could ask your family to follow Johnny Appleseed's example. You could all go together and shop for a small tree, then take along some shovels and ask the giftee where he or she would like the present planted. You could call it a "birthday tree" or even a "family tree"!

God planted lots of trees on earth. How many kinds of trees can you name?

What Is the Fastest-Growing Plant on Earth?

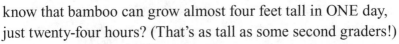

It's bamboo—a funny name for the fastest-growing plant on earth. Did you know that bamboo can grow almost four feet tall in ONE day, just twenty-four hours? (That's as tall as some second graders!)

For many years, bamboo has been used to make baskets, musical wind instruments, and fishing poles. (Ask your mom if she ever tried to catch a fish with a bamboo pole.) Today there are lots of fancier fishing poles, but now bamboo is being used in many other ways. Unlike some wood that is heavy and soft, properly treated bamboo forms a very hard "wood" that is lightweight but strong, so it can be used to make furniture or even some houses.

And recently, a company made a laptop computer with an outer case made of bamboo, and another company is making skateboards and snowboards from bamboo. And if your family ever brings Chinese takeout food home for dinner, it just might include some chewy bits of bamboo shoots. (Look in the Animal section of this book, and read about the panda, which eats bamboo for EVERY meal.)

Isn't it interesting that God made a plant that has young shoots tender enough to be used in delicious Chinese cooking but grows fast and becomes strong enough to be used to make a skateboard?

Don't be bamboozled (or hoodwinked) into believing it if somebody tells you that bamboo is just a funny-looking plant. You tell them that bamboo is a baffling, bewildering plant that can be used in a bazillion ways!

48

Did You Know There Are Two Kinds of Cat Tails?

If you or a friend has ever owned a kitty cat, you know that cats—skinny, fat, yellow, white, brown, or black—can be furry and purry AND they like to swish their tails around.

But did you know God also made a plant called cattail? It grows in marshy soil and has roots that grow rapidly and give strength to the soil, and its thick, leafy growth makes a safe place where nesting birds and other animals can shelter. Its tall, green leaves swish and wave in the breeze, a little like cat tails—and its "flower" doesn't look like a flower at all because it's about as round and as long as a velvety brown cat's tail! You might see cattails near a pond or a lake OR in a fancy bouquet because florists like to use this very unusual cattail "flower." (It feels a little bit furry but is never purry.)

If any of your classmates or neighborhood friends have kitty cats or other pets, it might be fun to have a pet show like the kind they often have on TV. You could go to a $1 store and buy some funny prizes, or you could make some blue-ribbon kind of awards, and maybe you could get some teenagers to be the judges. At the show, you could give prizes for the pets with the curliest tail, the warmest nose, the longest ears, the brightest feathers, or the saddest eyes. Do you think that might be a fun way to celebrate the fun fact that God made both cats and cattails?

49

Did You Ever Eat a Black-Eyed Pea?

Did you ever even SEE a black-eyed pea? It looks like a bean with a black eye. And some people think that eating black-eyed peas on New Year's Day will bring good luck. But some people think eating ANY kind of veggie is BAD luck.

And some others think it's fun that God made black-eyed peas and black-eyed Susans and black-eyed people.

What do YOU think?

50

Did You Ever Hear of Goulash, Shrimp Sinigang, or Slumgully?

These are funny names for delicious foods made with a mixture of vegetables. Evidently Jesus never ate any of these, but the Bible mentions he DID eat fish that the Apostles had caught, and he shared with his friends a Passover meal that included cooked lamb, unleavened bread, and herbs.

Jesus surely never heard of Hungarian goulash, which is a special stew made with spicy paprika, or shrimp sinigang, which sounds like a gang of friends singing while eating shrimp but is just a Filipino soup. Now slumgully is the name a mom gave to the yummy dish she concocted by adding a few spices to some leftovers. So Jesus just might have eaten a kind of slumgully his Mother stirred together.

Do you ever have a type of slumgully at YOUR house? Did you like it? Do you think Jesus would have liked it? He probably ate lots of vegetables, because many are grown in the area where he lived.

Aren't you lucky to have such a variety of foods to choose from in today's restaurants and markets—and such good cooks at your house to dish them up for you?

51

Do You Know What Nightshade Is?

Some people who have trouble sleeping might need a night-light to keep them safe from nightmares! Others might need a kind of nightshade—to cover their eyes and keep OUT the light. But there is a plant family known as the "deadly nightshades"—and they can be deadly or delicious! One of the most poisonous ones is called the jimsonweed. It has toothed leaves and spiny fruits and is sometimes called a thorn apple.

But one member of the nightshade family is called the POTATO! Yep, you have probably eaten one of the nightshades! Actually, all parts of the potato plant ARE poisonous except for the round brown taters that grow underground—and when they are dug up and cooked to make mashed potatoes or French fries, they are definitely delicious instead of deadly!

Another member of this family was once thought to be very poisonous until someone figured out that it was safe—and delicious too—and it's called the TOMATO, which is used to make ketchup to put on your French fries!

Aren't you glad it's safe to eat tomatoes and potatoes?

The next time you see something "new" on your dinner plate, "Try it...you might like it."

Did Your Family Ever Serve
a Bowl of Flowers for Dinner?

Maybe YOU wouldn't eat them, but the rest of the family probably would, because if you look closely you will see that broccoli and cauliflower are actually clusters of flowers! And an artichoke is a flower head. Do you LIKE broccoli or cauliflower or artichokes? What kind of vegetable do you like best—peas, beans, beets? Or do you just wonder why God made any kind of vegetable?

Do you think maybe God made them because they are GOOD for your health and God wants you to be good and healthy? And you know God made both white AND yellow corn so you could have corn on the cob. Now aren't you glad God made vegetables? The next time your family serves a bowl of flowers, try them so you can discover what it's like to eat flowers for dinner.

53

Did You Know That Grasses Cover Nearly One-Third of the Earth's Land?

And did you know God made many different kinds of grasses? There's orchard grass, canary grass, reed grass, meadow grass, and so forth. Grass grows on mountaintops, in valleys, and with all kinds of weather conditions. Grass grows on prairies, in forest glades, and on neatly tended lawns. If grazing animals such as sheep or goats nibble the grass down, it just grows back. And if a lawn mower cuts it down, it just grows back.

Do you know people who act like that? If someone "cuts them down" by saying something mean about them, they might be hurt, but they bounce right back. If they don't get something they wished for, they are disappointed, but they bounce right back. They are grateful for whatever good comes along and try to overlook the bad. Do you think that's a good way to be? Would you like to be like that?

54

Did You Ever See Grass on Your Breakfast Table?

If you ever ate cereal, you did! All the cereal grains—oats, wheat, rice, and even corn—come from "grasses." Oatmeal, corn flakes, and other popular "flake" cereals all begin as grass plants! Of course, the farmer has to grow them; harvest them; remove the wheat, oats, and so forth from the stalks and stems; and ship them to the cereal makers where they are processed (with maybe some sugar or fruit added) before they come to you in a box at the grocer's!

All these cereal grains began as wild-growing grass that dropped seeds that blew in the wind so more grass would grow each year. Then people began to try eating and cooking them and found out they were good, so they began saving seeds and today that's a big business. Some farmers collect the seeds and sell them to other farmers who plant new seeds every year instead of waiting for them to grow wild.

Would you like to be a farmer and live on a farm, or would you rather live in a city? God made each person different so there are some who like to plant, some who play music or paint pictures, some who are good at business, some who become priests or nuns, and some who become teachers or lawyers or grocers or cereal makers.

There are so many kinds of work to do—if we all do some kind of work and do it well, the world will work out just fine.

55

Do You Think Grass Could Grow Under Water?

Although grass is basically a land plant, there is one very special grass that grows in water. It's special because it's the MAIN food of more than half the humans who live on the earth. You know what it is? It's rice. Have you ever had chicken and rice soup or chicken and rice casserole or Rice Krispies dessert or some wonderful Asian foods made with rice? Then you know that rice is nice!

God also planted a "cousin" to white rice that is called wild rice, and the Indians in America once harvested it in canoes! They would bend the grassy rice stems over the canoe and knock the ripe rice grains into the bottom of the boat. Some of the grains would spill over the sides of the canoe and replant themselves so there would be more rice growing for the next year.

Doesn't that sound like fun, picking your dinner from a canoe? Actually, it was probably hard work, but it sounds like fun. One way you could "pick your dinner" without a canoe would be to go to a farmers' market where farmers sell fresh corn, tomatoes, peaches, strawberries, or whatever good food they have grown on their land. Ask your family if they would like to go shopping at that kind of market some day.

56

Did You Ever Find a Good Luck Four-Leaf Clover?

The clover plant normally has three leaves on a stem—and that might have been considered "good luck" by early Christians because they thought the three leaves stood for the Trinity—Father, Son, and Holy Spirit. But the four-leaf clover is considered good luck just because it's rare and you would hardly ever find one.

The clover plant itself is good luck or good fortune in several ways. First, its pink flowers are pretty enough to be used in a little bouquet, and they also attract bees that come and get nectar, which makes honey that people enjoy eating. The whole clover plant is also used to feed cattle, which like clover as much as people like honey.

And even the clover roots are special. They are like an underground fertilizer plant! The roots have little lumps of bacteria on them that somehow take nitrogen from the air and put it into the soil—which makes the soil rich and good for growing other things.

No wonder there's an old saying that suggests if you are having a good life, you're "living in clover"!

57

Do You Know What Plant Is Known as Nature's Candy Box?

The ancient Greeks once chewed on the pencil-thick roots of a plant they called simply "sweet root." Now we call it licorice.

Did you ever chew on a licorice stick? Today, these candy "sticks" are not the roots themselves but are made into candy using the flavor from the roots. They usually come in black or red, and you can take your pick of the sticks!

But licorice is not just a candy. Like many of the plants God made, it has lots more uses than just one! Licorice is also used in such different products as fire extinguishers, shoe polish, liquor, and cough drops! And there's even a musical instrument, the clarinet, that's nicknamed the licorice stick—probably because it makes such sweet-sounding music.

Do you like licorice or sweet-sounding music—or both?

Do You Know Where the Salt in a Saltcellar Comes From?

It sounds like it would come from the cellar or the basement, but cellar is just a fancy word for the saltshaker that probably sits on your kitchen table—and the salt in it may have come from the ocean or from a salt mine. Salt is a crystalline compound found in nature that is used to season vegetables and all kinds of food. Have you ever watched the cook in your family sprinkle salt and maybe pepper or herbs into whatever is cooking? Sometimes just a pinch of salt can make everything taste better.

Many years ago, salt was difficult to process, so it was very expensive. If there was a long dinner table with many people eating (as at a castle or an inn), a saltcellar would be put in the middle of the table. The important people were seated above it, near the head of the table, and they could help themselves to the salt. But less important people were seated "below the salt," and they were not allowed to use it!

Also many years ago, a Greek scholar wrote of discovering a "sweet salt" that the people of India prepared from a reedlike plant.

Today we call that "sweet salt" SUGAR, and the reedlike plant it comes from is SUGAR CANE. So you probably have a "sweet salt" or sugar bowl on your table next to the saltcellar—and you can help yourself to a spoonful of sugar or a pinch of salt whenever you want. Aren't you the lucky one!

59

Did Anyone Ever Tell You You're Full of Beans?

Being "full of beans" CAN be a compliment meaning you are full of enthusiasm. Or it could mean the person thinks you're full of nonsense. Or it could mean he or she thinks you sure do like to eat beans. Whichever the person means, it's OK. It's good to be enthusiastic, and sometimes nonsense is good too. And if you like to eat beans, you have LOTS of different kinds to choose from. First, there are jellybeans. But no, wait. Those are NOT vegetables.

The beans that ARE vegetables include green beans, lima beans, wax beans, kidney beans, chili beans, pork 'n' beans, navy beans, and baked beans. Beans are members of the large "legume" family, which also includes soybeans and peanuts. The soybeans have become very popular today, not just for making soy sauce for Chinese food but also for making substitutes such as soymilk and soy burgers. And the peanuts don't grow on a vine or bush like some beans but grow underground in peanut shells. That legume family sure has a long list of different kinds of relatives!

Do you have a big family? It can be fun to have a long list of different kinds of relatives. And when you all get together for a potluck supper, usually one of those delicious casseroles will be "full of beans"!

60

Do You Know the Difference Between a Green Pea and a Sweet Pea?

Well, a green pea is a delicious, nutritious vegetable that is used in many recipes. It grows in pods and has to be shelled before cooking. And there are also snow peas and sugar snap peas, which can be eaten, pod and all. You've probably seen some of those peas on your dinner plate.

But God also made the sweet pea, which is a flower that is pretty and pink and can grow faster and bloom longer than most wildflowers. The sweet pea pods look like the green pea pods but are a bit smaller and are NOT to be eaten. They could be poisonous to animals if they ate them in a large quantity.

But people are not likely to eat the seedpods and leaves of the flowers in their garden. Instead they just enjoy the beauty and the sweet scent of the climbing sweet peas that show their pretty faces in many backyards.

What kind of pea or bean is your favorite? What kind of flower is your favorite? Might it be a green pea AND a sweet pea?

Would You Like to See a Raspberry-Jam Tree?

If you wanted to see a raspberry-jam tree, you would have to go to Australia, and when you got there you might be disappointed. You might expect the tree to have jars of raspberry jam hanging from the tree the way apples hang from an apple tree. But no. It's just an ordinary tree when you look at it, but when you cut wood from it, the wood SMELLS just like raspberry jam—so that's the name they gave the tree.

In the same way, when you cut wood from a pine tree, it smells very piney. And when you cut branches from a lilac bush and burn them, you can smell the lilac odor just like the flowers smelled when they were hanging from the tree.

Well, maybe you don't like raspberry jam anyway. Maybe you'd rather have strawberry or grape jam, and you can get that at the grocery. But isn't it fun to know that one of God's trees was given such a delicious name?

Do You Ever Get in a Pickle?

If you get in a pickle, it means you are in trouble of some kind! It might even mean it's time to ask God to help you get out of some trouble. But just eating pickles will probably never get you in a pickle.

Did you know those pickles you like with a sandwich were made with the vegetable called a cucumber? Did you know a pickle is just a cucumber in disguise? Does this mean you've been eating a vegetable with your sandwich? Yes, it does.

When a cucumber is mixed with sugar, vinegar, and spices and cooked, it turns into a pickle. And if it's made properly, a pickle will make a crunch sound when you bite into one. In fact, the Pickle Packers International "Guide to Perfect Pickles" says that you should be able to hear that crunch at ten paces.

If you'd like to try the crunch test, you could get a friend to hold a pickle while you walk ten paces (big steps) away from him or her. Then get your friend to bite into the pickle, and see if you can hear the crunch. If you can, you've got a perfect pickle—and a delicious way to eat one of God's vegetables!

When Is a Saint Like a Spaghetti-Sauce Ingredient?

A saint and a spaghetti-sauce ingredient are alike because they have the same name— basil. Did you know there are several saints named Basil? One of them was known as Basil the Younger. He was a hermit who was arrested and tortured as a spy but was miraculously saved and released from prison and became famed for his miracles and holiness.

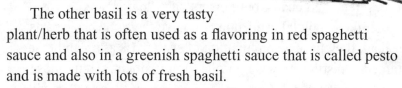

The other basil is a very tasty plant/herb that is often used as a flavoring in red spaghetti sauce and also in a greenish spaghetti sauce that is called pesto and is made with lots of fresh basil.

Do you know anybody who has the same name as a plant? Some girls have the same name as a flower—Daisy, Rose, Lily—and there IS a flower called sweet William, but guys don't have many flower or plant names. There ARE lots of people though who have been named after saints. How many do you know with a saint's name?

Did You Ever See a Flower?

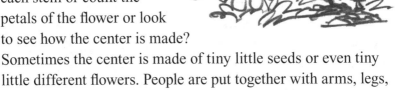

Well, duh! Of course, you have probably seen lots of flowers. But did you ever really SEE one? Did you ever look at one really closely to see how it's put together? Did you notice how many leaves are on each stem or count the petals of the flower or look to see how the center is made? Sometimes the center is made of tiny little seeds or even tiny little different flowers. People are put together with arms, legs, bodies, feet, and heads, but flowers have "parts" too.

Unlike people, flowers don't all have the same basic parts. Instead, they have a combination of such parts as an anther, a stamen, a pistil, a calyx, a corolla, or a filament. Aren't those funny names? A corolla sounds like a cigar, a filament sounds like part of a TV, and the anther sounds like the thing that comes after a question!

The next time you see a flower, try to really SEE it. Look to see how God put it together. And the next time you see another flower, see how it might be put together in a totally different way. God sure used his imagination when he made such a variety of flowers. And when God made you, he gave you some of that imagination. You shouldn't let it go to waste.

Some people are satisfied to spend too much time watching TV to see what somebody ELSE's imagination has put together. It's more fun to use your own imagination to come up with new ideas for today and for the future.

Do you ever do that?

65

Do You Know About Okra or Okefenokee?

Okra is a vegetable that some people think is delicious and others think is dastardly. Some like okra fried or pickled, in stews or in soups. Others like okra best when it is NOT anywhere near their dinner plate. And others grow okra just because it has such pretty red-centered yellow flowers.

Okefenokee is the name of a "wetlands" area that is a mix of bald cypress swamps, prairielike marshes, and quaking bogs (wet spongy ground). People who like to visit or study about swamps find the Okefenokee fascinating. Others just like the sound of that name—which simply means "shaking water."

Actually okra and Okefenokee have nothing in common except that both are green and they were both made by God—and it's kinda fun to say their names!

Did you ever eat okra or go to visit the Okefenokee? Do you ever wonder if you will ever learn about ALL the God-made wonders on the earth? Well, don't worry about that. Just be glad you will always have something to look forward to. Enjoy being a "super sleuth" so you can be surprised every time you discover another NEW fascinating fact.

When Are Garlic and a Tulip Flower Like a Light Bulb?

Sharp-smelling garlic and fresh-smelling tulips are very different, but they DO share something in common—they both grow underground from something called a bulb. You plant the bulb—which is shaped kinda like an electric light bulb—and one day you will have a beautiful flower called a tulip or a funny-smelling thing named garlic. The garlic could be called a vegetable OR an herb, and it's used in cooking to add an unusual but delicious flavor to foods. But if you ever plant a light bulb, do NOT expect it to grow into a lamp or a flashlight!

You probably know that a U.S. inventor named Thomas Edison came up with the idea for electricity and light bulbs, but did you know that when he was a young boy, his teacher thought he was too stupid even to be in school? In spite of that, he grew up to be a famous inventor. He produced 1,000 inventions, including the way to record voices and music—which led to today's recording of movies, TV shows, tunes on an iPod—and maybe even some e-mail homework lessons!

So if you ever think somebody is stupid (as Thomas Edison's teacher did) or think something is ugly (like a stinky garlic bulb), remember that God made every person and every thing for a good reason—and that includes YOU.

67

When There's a Bowl of Salted Peanuts on the Table, Can You Ever Eat Just One?

Most people find peanuts to be "habit-forming." If they ever eat just one, they want more. But did you know that it takes approximately 850 peanuts to make one standard-size jar of peanut butter? And did you know that if that was a GLASS jar of peanut butter and you recycled the jar, you could save enough energy to power your TV for three days?

Well, then you may want to get on the Internet and find the whole story of a black man named George Washington Carver. He was a U.S. scientist who spent years working with peanuts—and he researched 300 uses for this little goober!

When God made this delicious little treat, he designed a shell that looks like the crisscross design on an ice cream sugar cone. And God filled each shell with TWO peanuts (evidently knowing that nobody could eat just one!).

The next time you eat a peanut butter sandwich, see if you can come up with a list of different ways to use peanuts. It will be a sticky job, and you probably won't come up with 300 ideas—but it might remind you that something or somebody who is little can still do big things.

68

Have You Ever Heard the Words Crucifer or Cruciferous?

Crucifer and cruciferous look alike, but they are not. If you've ever seen a procession coming down the center aisle at church, you probably saw a man or maybe a boy or girl carrying a tall cross. Well, the one who carries the cross, especially at the head of a procession, is called a crucifer. Did you know that?

The word cruciferous has only three more letters added to the end, but it is used to describe a family of plants that include cabbage, turnips, and mustard. Bet you thought mustard was the yellow stuff you put on a hot dog. And you're right. It is. But it starts out as a leafy green plant that is sometimes boiled with a bit of ham or bacon to be served as a green vegetable. But the SEEDS of the mustard plant are ground into a powder that is used to make the yellow hot dog mustard!

Isn't it surprising how two words could be similar yet have such different meanings? It's the same with people. They can be similar, but God made each one oh-so-different. If you're ever waiting to meet someone—maybe at an airport or a restaurant—look around and notice how some are similar but none are exactly the same. Count how many have red hair or how many are wearing a blue shirt or how many are wearing lace-up shoes or how many are eating a hot dog!

Do You Like Bazooka, Dubble Bubble, or Wrigley's?

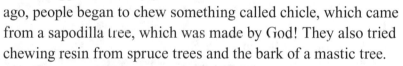

You probably know those are trade names for chewing gum, but did you know chewing gum was made by God? Well, not exactly—but sorta. Here's how it happened. Many years ago, people began to chew something called chicle, which came from a sapodilla tree, which was made by God! They also tried chewing resin from spruce trees and the bark of a mastic tree.

And do you know why people decided to chew part of a tree? Well, toothpaste hadn't been invented yet, so they hoped chewing gooey tree stuff would clean their teeth and freshen their breath. And besides, it was kinda fun.

Eventually, some people decided to experiment and find a way to make gum tastier, so they added flavors and rolled out strips of gum or shaped it into marble-sized rolls and even found a way to make chewing gum that would blow bubbles!

Today some dentists suggest you chew sugar-free gum to help clean your teeth just like the people who chewed sapodilla tree goo. And the U.S. military has been giving the troops chewing gum since World War I—to help relieve stress and improve concentration.

Does chewing gum improve your concentration, or is it just fun? What's your favorite gum to chew? Whichever it is, you can chew on the idea that gum came from trees, so you can thank God for making gummy trees.

70

Did You Ever Watch a Bodybuilder on TV?

Did you ever see a program about people who have exercised a lot and are called bodybuilders? Well, did you know that many foods are called bodybuilders too?

Bananas, dairy products, and green and yellow vegetables contain phosphorus, which is good for your nerves and muscles. Raisins, whole-grain cereals, beans, and leafy vegetables are rich in iron, which is good for your blood. And milk and dairy products are full of calcium that helps build your bones and teeth!

If you've eaten any of those foods, then you are a bodybuilder too!

Are you surprised to know you may have been eating iron, phosphorus, and calcium? Everyone knows that good cooks often stir in some "secret ingredient"—to make food delicious. Now you know that God also put some "secret ingredients" into your food—to make you strong and healthy. Aren't you glad he did?

71

What Plant Can Be Called by a Woman's Name or a Man's Name?

Herb can be a nickname for a man named Herbert—but it also describes flowering plants that can be used to flavor foods. The fragrant rosemary is one of them, along with parsley, oregano, marjoram, mint, sage, chives, thyme, and others. You've probably eaten a lot of delicious things that tasted so good because they were flavored with one of those plants.

Herbs can be grown in the garden or in little pots in the kitchen window. If you don't have home-grown ones, you can buy dried herbs in little containers at the grocery. When God planted vegetables to keep us healthy, he must also have realized we would like a little variety in our lives, so he added herbs.

Herbs are often mentioned in the Bible, and in the past there was a tradition that the herb thyme was mixed with the straw of the manger in Bethlehem, so many people always included a sprig of thyme when they put together Nativity crèches. And when there were knights defending kingdoms, thyme was considered a symbol of courage, so ladies would sew designs of thyme on the scarves they gave the knights to wear into battle.

The next time you taste some special recipe and you like the taste, ask the cook which herb was used in cooking it. The cook will know you don't mean which man named Herb!

Did You Ever Go to a Party That Had Chinese Lanterns?

Sometimes people have a Chinese New Year party where they serve Chinese food and decorate by hanging up a string of bright, beautiful, colorful Chinese lanterns. Other people have Chinese lanterns that grow in their garden!

This is a plant that is not very noticeable during most of the year. It's sorta boring-looking UNTIL autumn comes. Then it surprises everyone by blossoming forth with spectacular orange or blood-red "lanterns" that look like they are decorating the garden for a party.

Didn't God make lots of fun things to decorate his planet earth?

73

Where Could You Find Poison in Your Backyard?

Hopefully, you'll never find any there, BUT if you see a little innocent-looking green plant that has three leaves on one stem, DO NOT touch it. It's a plant called poison ivy that is NOT like the ivy that has one leaf on each stem and sometimes grows up the side of pretty brick buildings.

Now this plant is NOT poison like some mushrooms that will kill you if you eat them. But if you just touch any part of a poison ivy plant, it could make you miserable. In just a short time you can get a rash that will itch like crazy, and the rash will spread and the itching will last for what seems like a long time.

You can put different medicines on it, but you might have to go to a doctor to get the proper treatment to get rid of the itch.

Since each person's immune system is different, some people are more sensitive to this poison than others, but everyone has to be careful of it because nobody wants to risk that rash.

Most plants are our "friends," and most animals are too—but lions and tigers can be dangerous, and so can this poison ivy! Watch out for it—and let it be a reminder that there are other kinds of "poisons" that can make you miserable too—like somebody who tells lies and gets you in trouble or people who try to sell you drugs or "friends" who tell you it's OK to do something that you know is wrong.

Look out for that three-leafed ivy, and look out for "friends" who can lead you into itchy situations.

What's on Your Roof?

If it's December, it might be reindeer hoofprints, but if it's summertime, it might be fresh vegetables and herbs ready for the picking. In many cities, people don't have to go to a farm in the country to get fresh vegetables. They just go to the roof!

Some of the rooftop gardens are on business buildings and contain more flowers than veggies. Some apartment building roofs are filled with tomatoes, strawberries, and so on, which the people who live there have planted and will enjoy for dinner. And now schools are going to the roof too—to grow fresh vegetables that will be used in the school cafeteria.

All of these roof gardens are an environmental effort to help save God's good green earth.

Of course, you shouldn't try this on your house unless you have a very special kind of roof, because it has to be planned very carefully so the roof won't fall in, but you could maybe grow a small garden in your yard. You would be surprised at how different things taste when you have grown them yourself.

OR you could just imagine that you DO have a rooftop garden, and at dinnertime you could pretend that whatever vegetable you find on your plate has gone from the roof to the roof of your mouth! You could get your friends to play the pretend game with you, and after dinner you could call or text each other to find out who had what "roof-grown" vegetable and who liked which one better.

Minerals

(Anything That Is Not Animal or Vegetable!)

Diamonds and gold and silver,
Zinc and zircon, tin and titanium,
Airplane wings and spaceships.

75

Have You Ever Heard Any Rock Music?

If you've heard a waterfall splashing or some pebbles crunching under your feet when you walk along a path or the sound of a rock you've skimmed across a pond, you might call that "rock music." That's because those are sounds of the earth, and the earth is actually a really big rock! This rock is about 24,894 miles around and weighs more than six sextillion tons! That's a lot of rock. And it makes a lot of music!

Of course you don't see all the rock that is INSIDE the center of the earth. You SEE rocky mountains and rocks in a garden—plus the grass and trees and buildings and people that are all on the outside of the earth. And you know God planted some trees and plants and made animals and the people who later built the buildings. So now all of these things make "music" in many ways—with singing, talking, barking, meowing, or roaring voices plus drums and trumpets and the sound of the ocean lapping on the shore or a breeze moving through a tree.

Aren't you glad God made the earth that makes all those special kinds of "rock" music?

76

Do You Know What Bulletproof Vests, Fire Escapes, Windshield Wipers, and Laser Printers Have in Common?

They are all made with different kinds of minerals and metals—AND they were all invented by women!

These are all lifesavers in different ways. You would be glad to have a bulletproof vest if you joined the police force and someone was shooting at you. And you would be lucky to find a fire escape if you were in a building that caught fire. Now you may never need to wear a bulletproof vest or climb down a fire escape, but you probably WILL ride in a car with windshield wipers—and they might save your life by helping the driver see the road better in a big rainstorm.

But what about a laser printer? If you do your homework on a computer and need to print it out in hurry, you might feel like the printer had "saved your life" by printing clearly and quickly.

So why don't you say a prayer today to thank God for all the inventive women—and men—who invented things using minerals and metals, things that just MIGHT save your life!?

How Is a Rock Like a Birthday Cake?

A birthday cake might be like a rock if you let the cake get stale and hard, but how would a rock ever be like a birthday cake?

If you ever made a birthday cake or watched someone make one, you would notice that a cake is made of a MIX of ingredients—like eggs, flour, milk, and maybe chocolate, all stirred together before you bake it. Well, most rocks are a mixture too—made of one or more minerals "stirred" together in different ways.

For example, granite includes the minerals quartz and feldspar. You may have seen granite in a kitchen (where you make cakes) because a lot of kitchen countertops are made of granite.

But plain old rocks are EVERYWHERE, so watch for interesting rocks wherever you go. When you pick up a rock, look it over carefully and see if you think it might be made of many ingredients—and think about how God made all these rocks and minerals and stirred them together so you could discover them. Some people have a hobby of collecting different types of rocks. Would you like to try that?

Ahoy! Do You Know What an Alloy Is?

Rocks are not the only minerals that are all mixed up! People have found ways to mix up God's minerals, and, when they do, it's called an alloy.

For example, believe it or not, iron is a rather soft mineral so it can't be used alone to build some things. Instead, iron is mixed with manganese and phosphorus while all are in a molten state (melted by heat). This mix becomes the alloy called steel, which is strong enough to build the framework of tall skyscrapers.

Gold is also too soft to make certain things, so it's mixed with a bit of copper to become another alloy.

A little boy once suggested you could try to make an alloy by mixing pancake flour with popcorn so the pancake could flip itself! But don't try this in YOUR kitchen. It might get you mixed up in a lot of trouble.

79

Did You Know All Rocks on Earth Are Divided Into Three Large Groups?

Yep—and these groups have fancy names. The three are sedimentary, igneous, and metamorphic.

Igneous rocks are named from the Latin word that means "fiery" because they begin as magma, the molten hot material that is in the earth's interior. When magma hardens underground, it cools slowly to form granite and other coarse-grained rocks.

Sedimentary rocks are made up of "sediments," things that settle down and get hard and turn into stone. (Did you ever try to put sugar into iced tea? Some of it settles down to the bottom of the glass, and, after you drink the tea, the sugar crystals turn into a hard sediment.)

Metamorphic rocks happen when rocks are under very strong heat or pressure (maybe as a hamburger might turn into something that looks like a piece of charcoal if you pressed down on it with the spatula too long on a very hot grill). Sometimes one kind of rock turns into a different kind the way limestone, under heat and pressure, can turn into marble—the kind of "rock" used to make beautiful statues!

If you could go on the Internet or look at an encyclopedia at the library, you could find pictures of the way God made rocks so they can change and turn into something new. Would you like to turn into something new? You can, you know. If you try, you can always turn into something BETTER!

80

What Would You Use in a Kitchen, on an Airplane, and at a Pigeon Race?

Here's a hint: it comes from bauxite (which is a combination of minerals), and it's the most abundant metal found in the earth's crust. And its name is aluminum. You've probably seen it in your kitchen when your dad is cooking something in an aluminum pot or your mom is wrapping something in aluminum foil to put in your lunch.

Thousands of years ago, the people who lived in Iraq discovered that there was a lot of aluminum mixed in the kind of clay that was in the ground in their country. They learned how to beat it into very thin sheets and use those sheets to make cooking pots. Many years later, in the early 1900s (still years before you were born) someone in France figured out how to press aluminum between very heavy rollers and turn it into foil similar to the kind used today to wrap up leftovers or to cover a bowl of potato salad to take to a picnic.

Still much later, it was discovered that aluminum was a great material to use to make airplanes because it is very light yet very strong.

And what about those pigeon races? Well, Americans FIRST used aluminum foil when it was a popular sport to have races with homing pigeons. Each pigeon's owner would take a band of aluminum foil with a number on it and wrap it around the pigeon's leg to identify it. The aluminum foil would not melt like paper if it was raining, and it was strong enough not to fly off in a strong wind so it would travel safely through the race. And when the first pigeon came back and landed, they could look at the number and know who won the race!

Isn't it amazing how God put minerals in the crust of the earth and then gave people brains smart enough to find so many ways to use them—to help with such different things as kitchens, airplanes, and pigeons!

81

Did You Ever Ride a Dandy Horse?

Maybe you have—if you've ever ridden a bicycle. Many years ago, a man named Baron Sauerbronn invented something he called a "dandy horse." It had two wheels joined by a rod with a seat on top and a steering thing so you could go straight ahead or turn right or left. But it did NOT have any pedals, so you had to push it along with your feet. Evidently it was faster than walking because maybe you could hold up your feet once you got on a roll, but that doesn't sound very dandy—it didn't have a brake!

A few years later someone improved the design by adding pedals and gears, but these "horses" were nicknamed "bone-shakers" because the seats had no springs. You got all-shook-up every time the bike hit a bump.

Soon, year by year, others kept adding more improvements, and by 1890 bicycles had rubber tires, coaster brakes, and handlebars. Today bikes have headlights, horns, reflectors, different speeds, special suspensions, and so forth.

Ever since the dandy horse, bikes have been made of some kind of mineral or metal, and today frame materials include carbon fiber, titanium, and aluminum.

But do you know the most important improvement made for today's bikes? It's called a bicycle helmet! You should ALWAYS wear one so it can protect that dandy head God made just for you. You wouldn't want to fall and mess up one of God's most special creations, would you?

82

Could There Be a Patron Saint for Computers?

If you ever looked inside a computer, you would see lots of wires and whatchamacallits—made of many different kinds of minerals, metals, and thingamajigs. This will give you a clue so you would know why so MANY things can sometimes go wrong with your e-mail or homework!

That's why computers and computer users NEED a patron saint. And it isn't a surprise to hear that it's Saint Isidore of Seville, who was one of the smartest, most learned men of the time when he lived (he even put together an encyclopedia!). But even more important, he was also one of the holiest men—and that's why he's called a saint.

So the next time a computer glitch makes you dizzy, ask Saint Izzy to help you download a solution.

(Since there are many patron saints, you might like to know some of the ones who fit the "mineral" category. The patron saint of coppersmiths is Saint Maura; patron of blacksmiths, Saint Dunstan; patron of metalworkers, Saint Eligius; patron of sculptors, Saint Claude; patron of stonemasons, Saint Barbara.)

Do You Know the Name of the First Human-Made Satellite?

It was a historic, heroic event in 1957 when Russia's SPUTNIK became the first human-made "spaceship" to be launched into orbit.

Since then, there have been lots of spacecrafts launched by the United States and other countries, men have walked on the moon, and there has even been a space station launched and LEFT in space.

When you see spaceships in movies or on TV, they sometimes look shiny—as if they are made of that aluminum foil in your kitchen. There probably is some aluminum in a spaceship PLUS lots of other minerals PLUS the "animals" known as astronauts and also some vegetable products to feed those astronauts. It takes a LOT of animal, vegetable, and mineral stuff to put a spaceship into orbit.

Do YOU ever "go into orbit" when something makes you mad? What do you do to "come back down to earth"? The next time you feel mad, do you think it might help to send a prayer into orbit, asking God for a happy landing?

Try it—instead of going sputniking all over the place.

84

Did You Ever See a Picture of a Volcano?

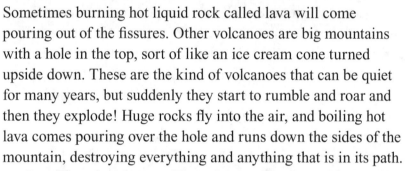

Volcanoes are pretty exciting—but they can do a lot of damage too. Some volcanoes are gently sloping mountains that have cracks called fissures in them. Sometimes burning hot liquid rock called lava will come pouring out of the fissures. Other volcanoes are big mountains with a hole in the top, sort of like an ice cream cone turned upside down. These are the kind of volcanoes that can be quiet for many years, but suddenly they start to rumble and roar and then they explode! Huge rocks fly into the air, and boiling hot lava comes pouring over the hole and runs down the sides of the mountain, destroying everything and anything that is in its path.

But, like a lot of scary things that happen, something good can come along later. After the volcano stops erupting and all the lava turns cold, it leaves lots of minerals thrown up from deep inside the earth. Some of the lava can be used as building material, and pumice (a byproduct of lava) can be used as a grinder and polisher and in the building of roads. The soil from decayed volcanic material is rich in minerals so it can be used in farming to produce good harvests.

Did you ever have something bad happen that was very scary—but then something good came later? Do you ever rumble and roar and then explode and throw around some red-hot mean words? After you calm down, do you say you're sorry and make up with whomever you hurt? That's one way to make something good come out of something scary.

How Do Peanuts, Clover, or Alfalfa Help Farmers?

Did you know a farmer has to be sure to have the proper amount of minerals in the soil he uses to grow things? And every year the crop he grows uses up some of the minerals, so he has to be sure to put more back in or his new crops will get smaller and smaller every year.

So some farmers plant alternate crops of clover, peanuts, and alfalfa because these plants put nitrogen back into the soil. Farmers especially like alfalfa because it's hardy and can live through long dry spells with roots that sink deep into the earth to reach moist earth and water, PLUS the alfalfa can also be used as food for their animals.

Isn't it amazing how God made plants that can help each other? Have you noticed that some people—grandmas, neighbors, teachers, school friends—are like that too?

Whom do you know like that—someone who always tries to help others? Do YOU ever try to help others?

86

Did You Know That Sand Comes in Different Colors?

If you've ever had fun playing in a sandbox, the sand was probably a light tan color. If you've ever run in the sand by the ocean, the sand might have been white. But sand can also be black or even pink.

Sand is a mineral mix of quartz, feldspar, and mica—tiny bits of rocks that have been washed down a mountain by rain. But in Hawaii, you might see black beach sand that's called basalt rock, made by volcanic ash that came from black lava. In Florida, you might see white sand made of bits of coral rock or pink sand made of bits of pink seashells.

And did you know that sand can be used in many ways—to make mortar or concrete or even glass? Bet you thought sand was just for running barefoot on the beach or building sandcastles.

Like so many of God's creations, sand can be very useful—but fun too!

87

Do You Know What the First Lawn Mower Looked Like?

It probably looked like a sheep or a goat or any kind of animal that liked to eat grass! But now there are all kinds of lawn mowers made of metals, so today grass-eaters could fit into both the animal AND mineral categories! The first push-mower was probably invented in 1830 when an Englishman named Edwin Budding attached metal blades to a cylinder that turned around as it was pushed and chopped up the grass. Much later, other inventors found a way to add a gasoline or an electric motor to the push-mower, and trimming the grass got easier. Today there are even power mowers you can ride to cut larger lawns. But there are still places where hungry animals have the job of mowing the grass.

When God planted grass on the earth, he left it up to people to figure out how to use it to make nice lawns AND how to mow it to keep it from growing higher than an elephant's eye! Maybe someday you will be asked to help your family by mowing the lawn.

What jobs could you do today to help your mom, dad, grandparents, or neighbors?

CHOMP

Did You Ever Find a Copper?

Some people think it's good luck to find a copper penny—especially if it's a brand-new shiny one. You can often find one on a sidewalk, in a parking lot, or anywhere that somebody might have dropped one. Since these coins are made with copper, a bright shiny mineral, they sometimes catch your eye with the sparkle. But they've been used in the United States for so many years that the often-used ones usually turn into a dull brown color.

Since pennies are only worth ONE cent, some people don't like to carry around a lot in their pockets so they "collect" pennies in a jar until they have enough to trade in for dollars. Some people who collect all kinds of coins as a hobby check each penny because some of the older ones are worth lots of money.

In some places, people are so poor that to find one penny or any kind of coin would be very good luck.

Have you ever found a penny? The next time you find any kind of coin, why don't you start collecting them in a box or jar, and, when you get enough, you could donate them to someone who would feel very lucky to get any kind of coin collection.

89

Where Could You Find a Whole Lot of Gold in the United States?

Near Fort Knox, Kentucky, more than four million TONS of gold is stored. It's called the United States Bullion Depository.

Why there is so much there? Until the 1930s, gold coins were used as money in the United States, but then the government decided not to use gold coins and asked everyone to exchange his or her gold for dollars. The coins were weighed, and people received $20.67 for each ounce of gold.

Then the government needed a safe place to keep all this gold, so they built the Depository, a fortresslike structure with a vault lined with granite walls, protected by a blast-proof door that weighs twenty-two tons. They also stored some other valuable things with the gold such as the original U.S. Declaration of Independence and the U.S. Constitution because this Depository was considered to be so safe. After that, people would say things like "This is as safe as Fort Knox" or "It's locked up tighter than Fort Knox."

Do you have some favorite things you think are valuable—like a special rock or seashell or book or medal or rosary? Do you have a safe place to keep them—like a box or shelf or dresser drawer? If you don't, you might like to make a "Fort Knox" kind of place where you can save your treasures and know they will be there, when you want to take them out and look at them or show them to a friend.

And when you say your prayers at bedtime, you could thank God for all the PEOPLE who are "treasures" in your life.

90

Where Could You Find Gold in Your Neighborhood?

You might try looking at the left hand of all the women you know. Many of them wear golden rings they received on the day of their wedding. This lovely real gold never rusts, and it is so soft you can beat it into thin sheets or pull it out into a wire. And it's very valuable. Although it's used to make elegant jewelry, it's also used in connectors for electronic equipment. And in the past it was used for coins. You can see a lot of beautiful ancient golden coins in museums.

You can also see lots of beautiful golden decorations in the cathedrals and Catholic churches all across Europe and the Americas. Many of them are hundreds of years old, but the gold still glows. People who built those churches wanted to use the very best materials to honor God, so they used colorful stained-glass windows and elegant architecture, and, of course, they had golden chalices on the altars. Most of these expensive decorations were donated by rich people who wanted to share their wealth. And their gifts have offered inspiration to several generations of people—rich or poor, young or old, parishioners or visitors.

Did you ever hear the saying, "Silence is golden?" It's nice to have fun with your friends, but sometimes it's very nice to go someplace where you can be very quiet—like maybe your backyard or your church—and spend some time all alone, just thinking about God and listening to see whether God has a message for you.

When you spend time talking to God, silence IS golden.

What Does Paul Revere Have to Do With "Silver Bells"?

Not much, really, but Paul Revere was a famous silversmith, which meant he made lots of things out of silver—like maybe silver bells! He also is a famous American who warned the patriots that the British were coming and maybe helped turn the tide of the Revolutionary War. A man named Henry Wadsworth Longfellow even wrote a poem that begins, "Listen, my children, and you shall hear/Of the midnight ride of Paul Revere."

Did you ever hear that poem, or did you ever hear little silver bells ding-a-linging or BIG silver bells ding-donging?

Well, there are a lot of connections with silver because it is a precious metal that has been used by people all over the world since ancient times. If someone is a very good speaker, you might say that person is "silver-tongued." If someone's family has always been very rich, you might say, "She was born with a silver spoon in her mouth."

Silver has been used to make spoons plus knives and forks and very fancy dishes and doodads. Some people collect those pieces especially if they have been "handed down" through the family—like Grandma's pretty silver teapot.

Silver was once also used to mean money because coins were made from it, but most of today's "silver" coins are made from a mixture of copper and nickel.

And did you know the patron saint of silversmiths is Saint Andronicus? So if you want to tell someone about silver, you can talk about a saint with an unusual name or Paul Revere or spoons or teapots or coins—and maybe they will think you are silver-tongued!

92

Do You Know What Is Bright Red and Has Eight Sides?

You probably see one when you're on your way to the movies or to school or to get some pastafazool. It is on many street corners, and the big red metal sign has white letters that spell STOP.

This is a reminder that you should stop and let someone else have a turn.

Not too many years ago, there were no stop signs because there were only horses and carriages on the roads, and horses can't read signs. Today there are lots of automobiles and lots of people in a hurry! If there were no stop signs, cars would be running into each other all the time.

Many years ago, God put up some "stop signs" too—and they're called the Ten Commandments. You should ask someone in your family to tell you all about them. They are simply ten rules to follow to lead a good and happy life. Just like traffic signs, the Ten Commandments keep people from running into trouble.

Next time you're in a hurry and want people to get out of your way or the next time you're just about to say something mean to someone, think about God's STOP sign. Stop before you do or say something you might be sorry for later.

(And just in case you never ate any, pastafazool is a delicious Italian pasta recipe. When you're eating it, you might NOT want to STOP!)

93

Got a Nickel in Your Pocket?

Did you know nickel is a silvery-white metallic element that is used in alloys—but it's also what we call a U.S. five-cent piece? In spite of being called a nickel, this coin is made of only about 25 percent nickel and 75 percent copper!

And did you know a nickelodeon was once the name of a movie theater where admission usually cost a nickel? And did you know a nickelodeon is also another name for a jukebox, which is another name for a coin-operated machine that plays music and is sometimes found in small restaurants?

And did you know that frosty cola drinks once cost only a nickel, so there was a radio commercial that began with people singing, "Nickel, nickel, nickel, trickle, trickle, trickle..." to make you think how good it would feel to have a frosty cola trickling down your throat—and it would cost only a nickel.

Well, now you know that at one time, if you had a nickel in your pocket, you could go to a movie, put a nickel in a machine that would play your favorite song, or treat yourself to a frosty cold drink. What could you do with a nickel today?

Well, you could put it in a little box and keep adding nickels until you had enough to exchange for a dollar bill. Then the next time you go to church and they pass a collection basket, you could drop in your own dollar and think about all the ways the Church uses dollars to help needy people. Nickel, nickel, nickel, trickle, trickle trickle....

94

Would You Ever Have a Quarrel About a Quarry?

Well, probably not. If someone ever inquires or asks you about a quarry, you can just tell them it's a huge pit where rocks are cut or blasted out of the ground. Who could quarrel with that?

But you could also tell them that, as long ago as prehistoric times, people were digging in quarries to get flint or sharp rocks they could attach to sticks to use as weapons or tools. Today, explosives are used in quarries to blast out tons of rock at a time. Then the rock is scooped up by huge bulldozers and taken to be crushed or ground into stones that can be used to make roads, concrete, or cement. If the rock is to be used in building or paving, instead of blasting, electric cutters, wire saws, and drills are used to cut the stone into larger blocks.

A lot of those blocks are used to build malls, grocery stores, schools, and churches. Isn't it amazing how rocks in a hole in the ground can be used for so many different things?

95

Do You Know Anyone Who Has a Lead Foot?

You probably do, because that's what they say about someone who likes to drive a car fast—sometimes too fast! It seems like that person's foot is as heavy as lead when he or she pushes down hard on the gas pedal and takes off in a big hurry!

Actually, lead is an old and important metal. It has been used in making bullets, batteries, and lots of lead pipes. And in recent years, it has been used to make radiation shields. (Did you ever go to the dentist and have x-rays taken of your teeth? If you did, you may remember they put a very heavy covering over you to protect you from the radiation of the x-rays. It's heavy because it's made of lead.)

The Latin name for lead is *plumbum,* which is probably the reason people who know how to fix pipes are called plumbers! And lead pipes are so strong, they last a long time. Some that are still in use in Italy have the insignia of Roman emperors on them—which means they could have been there about the same time as the Apostles!

Now here's a little project for you. Lead is so old it's even mentioned in the Bible in the Book of Exodus, chapter 15, verse 10. So why don't you "get the lead out" and look that up to see what the Bible says about lead?

96

Did You Ever Wear or See a Quartz Watch?

Did you know that quartz is a rock-forming mineral that might be found in igneous or metamorphic rocks? Pure quartz is as clear as glass, but sometimes it gets mixed with other minerals and changes color. Traces of titanium can change it into rose quartz, and small amounts of iron turn it into the purple variety known as amethyst. Amethyst is considered a semiprecious gem and is often used in jewelry. Quartz crystals are used in electronic clocks and watches, which are known for keeping very accurate time.

Lots of minerals mix up with each other and make interesting things such as semiprecious gems and crystals for a watch.

Do you like to mix up things? Have you ever tried making banana soup? Just let some vanilla ice cream melt a bit, and while it's melting chop up a banana. Mix up the two and you have banana soup. Or you could just mix up peanut butter and jelly and make a PBJ sandwich. If it's a warm day, you could take your soup or sandwich outside and sit under a tree, and while you eat you could look around and count all the things you see that were made by God. You could start with the banana or the peanut!

It's Real Quartz!

What's a Good Name for a Battleship?

During the World War II era, battleships were given the names of states, and one of them was named the *Missouri*. When the war ended, Harry Truman was president of the United States and he was from Missouri, so that battleship was chosen to be the place where leaders would meet to sign a peace pact. Did you know that?

A battleship is made of many minerals and usually carries many soldiers plus lots of food to feed the soldiers, so it would fit into the animal OR vegetable OR mineral category!

Wouldn't it be a happier world if we did not need any battleships or battlegrounds or war? Think about that the next time you get sooo mad you want to wage war with someone or start a battle.

98

Did You Ever See a Movie or Read a Book About Pirates?

Often in a movie or book, there will be a time when the pirates open up a big treasure chest and inside there are lots of shiny, sparkling jewels. Wouldn't that be exciting? Even in the Bible, there are stories of important men wearing "breastplates" decorated with gems such as emeralds, sapphires, and diamonds. But did you know that most of the most special stones called gems are minerals!

There are rich red rubies, deep green emeralds, bright blue sapphires, and, of course, those glittering, glistening diamonds. These are the royalty of the mineral world, the most valuable "stones." And they can be found all over the world. The finest emeralds are mined in South America. The best rubies come from Burma, high-quality sapphires are found chiefly in Asia, and South Africa is known for diamonds. The Kimberley mine there dug up more than three TONS of diamonds, and the largest diamond ever found came from its Premier mine.

Did you ever see any of these minerals? You could go to a museum and see ancient jewelry in exhibits like the ones found in King Tut's tomb, or you could go to England to see exhibits of the royal jewels still worn today by the Queen of England. Or you could just look around and see gems in the jewelry your friends or family wear—rings, earrings, necklaces, bracelets, and so forth. Lots of them are REAL gems, but today some jewelry is made of pretty but not "precious" stones.

God put jewels in the earth for people to dig them up and enjoy the beauty of the "jewels," but he also made people smart enough to find a way to make imitation gems so everyone can afford to wear "jewels." And isn't that great!

(If you're ever in a jewelry store, you can get loopy if you ask to see their loupe—a small magnifier that fits over an eye and is used by jewelers and watchmakers to determine which are REAL jewels.)

99

Did You Ever Hear of the Element Iridium?

Probably not, because it's extremely rare on the surface of the earth—but, according to a recent newspaper story, it IS plentiful in meteorites. Evidently meteorites often streak across the sky, coming from outer space. Many of them are vaporized before they get here, but some DO land on earth—and leave traces of iridium.

Scientists test layers of the earth for levels of iridium to help them figure out how long it took for a layer of earth to form. It makes a difference if there's a lot or a little iridium.

Did you know the earth had layers? Did you know meteorites streak across the sky? Did you know scientists test a lot of strange things? Would you like to be a scientist someday and do lots of tests?

Here's a test for you today. Can you name the seven sacraments of the Church? If you can, very fast, that's very good. If you can but it takes a long time, that's still good. How fast do you think the iridium-testing scientists could name them?

100

Did You Ever Play a Game With a Taw?

Some people like to collect marbles—like the sculptures you might see in a museum that are made out of a beautiful white stone called marble. Other people like to collect a different kind of marble—little round glass balls that are very pretty too with designs of strips and jiggles of colors.

These balls are used in a game that's simply called shooting marbles, and the ball you use to shoot at the other marbles is called a taw! Did you ever play the game of marbles? If you didn't, you should ask your parents or grandparents to tell you about it.

The kind of marble that's used for statues you might see in church usually looks pure white, but sometimes it just seems like that until you take a close look and see that it has little jiggles of color or shadings in it too. There is also a marble cake, named that way because it has jiggles of both vanilla and chocolate.

Would you rather go to a museum or play a game or eat cake? That might be a hard-as-marble decision, since they all sound like fun.

Which Are More Important—Glamorous Minerals or Hard-Working Ones?

Most people might think the glamorous jewels, which are very sparkly and beautiful, would be the more important. But the hard-working metallic metals have played a bigger role in human history. Ever since early humans figured out how to make tools and weapons from bits of copper and iron, the search to find more uses for metals has continued until today.

Approximately 3,000 minerals exist in nature, and people are constantly finding new commercial ways to use the hard-working ones—from building materials to the latest technologic things such as iPods, cell phones, and computers. And where do they find these hard workers?

The mineral galena is the richest source of lead. The bright red cinnabar contains mercury, and cassiterite is the main source of tin-bearing ore. And iron, probably the most important metal of all because of the many ways it's used, comes from deposits of hematite.

Did you ever hear of hematite or galena or cassiterite?

You've probably heard of cinnamon buns but maybe not cinnabar. Are you surprised at all the kinds of things God buried in the earth and the many ways people have found to use them?

Do you think maybe people may be like minerals—the glamorous ones are not always as important as the hard-working ones?

102

What Does Carbon Have to Do With Carbonated Colas?

You've probably had a carbonated cola or soda with your sandwich for lunch, but did you know what made it into a fizzy, bubbly, fun-to-drink beverage? Well, it contains something called carbon dioxide— which comes from carbon.

Carbon is an important element that is present in every living thing—both plant and animal. A lot of things we use every day have carbon in them—such as sugar and paper. And the "lead" in a pencil we use to write on that paper is actually a form of carbon called graphite, a name that comes from a Greek word that means "to write." Other forms of carbon include coal, oil, diamonds, and the carbon dioxide that is used in making life jackets, air guns, paintball markers—and that fun, fizzy, carbonated drink!

And oh, yes, carbon dioxide is also used in making Pop Rocks, the candy that "explodes" in your mouth!

So the next time you have fizzy candy or cola or play paintball or write with a pencil, celebrate carbon, one of the many wonders of God's world.

103

Do You Know What a Lodestone Is?

You probably have one on your refrigerator door. Yes, it's a magnet! A magnet is "attracted" or drawn to metal such as iron or steel (or a refrigerator door), and it will stick to the metal. But this kind of small magnet is just a small part of the magnetic story.

Computer information or TV programs are often stored by using a magnetic recording process. And doctors diagnose some medical problems by using something called magnetic resonance imaging or MRI to produce computerized pictures of the body. And people who like to go hiking or exploring take along a compass so they won't get lost, because the compass has a magnetic needle that will always point north and show them which direction to take to get back home.

The compass needle points north because the axis of the earth points to the North Star, which is called a polestar or a lodestar—a star that leads or guides. A person is also sometimes called a lodestar—meaning someone who leads, guides, and is an inspiration or role model. That kind of person has a magnetic personality!

Do you know anyone who is a lodestar? Are you inspired to follow that person's example? Did you know you too could be a lodestar if you are always guided by God's teachings and are drawn to him by his magnetic love and joy?

Open a Window, and What Do You See?

If you live in the mountains, you might see snowy tree branches. If you live in the tropics, you might see a sandy beach. Or if you use a computer, you might be opening a Windows operating system!

Of course, you know that your house windows are made from glass, which surprisingly, is made from sand, soda, and limestone (all made by God). And the Windows in your computer are made with some kind of minerals (which were also made by you-know-Who).

When you see glass in the window of your bedroom, it's a solid, but before that it was a molten hot liquid that was poured into molds and cooled to make your windowpane. That hot liquid can also be blown into different shapes by expert glass blowers.

Glass is used to make bottles, drinking glasses, eyeglasses, mirrors, light bulbs, and lots and lots of other things. It's easy to see that glass makes a big difference to your everyday life.

And best of all, glass lets you see through walls!

105

Did You Ever Hear About Tom Sawyer and Titanium?

There's a popular book about a boy named Tom Sawyer who is always exploring and getting into trouble—and one chapter tells about a day when Tom's aunt gives him the job of painting a white picket fence. Soon Tom gets tired of painting so he tricks his friends into doing it for him by convincing them it will be sooo much fun.

Now what does that have to do with titanium? This important metal is used in aircraft, spacecraft, guided missiles, and rockets where strength must be combined with lightness. But titanium can also be used as a cutting tool, in jewelry—and in white paint! What a combination—from spaceships to white paint. Tom would have loved that.

You wouldn't ever try to trick someone into doing your work, would you? That's not a good idea, but it IS a good idea to read books about boys like Tom who have a lot of adventures and a lot of fun.

The next time you see a white-painted fence or a rocket, wonder whether either or both of them might contain that amazing mineral known as titanium, made by God!

106

What Does Tuna Fish Have to Do With a War Ship?

The tuna fish for your sandwich comes out of a "tin can," and a destroyer—a small, fast warship usually used to support larger vessels and often armed with five-inch guns, depth charges, torpedoes, and even guided missiles— is sometimes called a "tin can"!

Tin is one of the oldest metals known and has many uses. Actually the tin cans for food—such as tuna and soups—are not made entirely of tin. Tin is the thinner-than-paper coating on the steel surface of the can that keeps it from rusting. And it takes a lotta tin to make a lotta cans—about fifty billion cans a year!

Did you know an early automobile—the Model T Ford— was nicknamed the Tin Lizzie? And a person who can't carry a tune when singing might be said to have a tin ear? And at weddings, sometimes friends will tie tin cans on the back of the car that belongs to the bride and groom so that, when they leave the wedding, the cans will bounce around against each other and make a lot of noise—just for fun?

Have you ever seen a destroyer or a Tin Lizzie or a wedding?

The next time you're have a tuna sandwich for lunch, think about all the uses for tin, and make a list of all the things you think might be put in those fifty billion tin cans.

107

Check Out the Heckelphone and the Oh-Boy Oboe!

Most people have never heard of a heckelphone unless they are musicians. It's actually similar to the oboe, which is a woodwind instrument. Most people HAVE heard of the word "heckle," which means to bother someone who is speaking or teaching or making an announcement. The heckler will interrupt or ask stupid questions or make fun of what the speaker is saying— which is very rude. But the heckelphone was not named for a heckler but for those who invented it—Wilhelm Heckel and his sons. And the oboe might have been named when someone who liked its music said, "Oh boy, let's call it an oboe." Who knows?

Do you or would you like to play a musical instrument? Music has been an important part of life all through history.

The Bible mentions musical instruments, and very early paintings show people playing pipes, harps, and other stringed instruments that look like violins. Since then, many people have invented new ways to make music. In addition to the woodwinds, there are brass winds, strings, and percussions. There are also music-makers named bassoons, piccolos, trombones, drums, tambourines, French horns, tubas, and so forth, and sometimes they all play together in something called a symphony. In recent years, people have also invented electronic instruments such as the synthesizer, electric guitar, and so forth.

Music always adds "something" to movies, TV shows, parties, or any kind of get-together. And there are lots of different kinds of music: rock, jazz, blues, folk, soul, rap, and country/western. What musical instrument would you like to play? Would it maybe be the heckelphone?

Do You Know the Name of the Third Rock From the Sun?

The third "rock" or major planet from the sun is called Earth—and YOU can call it home. As far as anyone knows, the Earth is the ONLY planet where people and plants and animals can live. Some 70 percent of the Earth is covered by water, and it has one natural satellite called the MOON—but you knew that, didn't you?

Did you ever go to a planetarium to see how your home planet is different from other planets and how they all move around in the atmosphere, the stratosphere, the thermosphere, the ionosphere, and so forth? It's amazing to see how God put all that together.

Today many people think your home planet needs help because the people who live here have been wasting a lot of things and mistreating the planet. Maybe you could make a

Save-the-Planet poster or maybe you could have a Planet-Savers Contest with your family or friends.

See who can think up the most ideas of things to do to help the planet. For example, you could bike or walk short distances to save fuel, stack and bundle newspapers and take them to a recycling bin, recycle empty soda cans, or look around and see if you have any old computer parts or printers or any kind of technologic things that your family no longer uses and take them to a recycling center.

OR you could get together a group of kids and go to businesses in your area and ask what they are doing to save the environment. If you find some who are working on this, you could present each of them with a poster that says, "The Save-A-Planet Kids Club presents this award to (name of store) for working to Save Our Planet!"

What Toys Go Around in the Best Circles?

These metallic toys are sometimes saved and passed down through generations. It starts when a boy or girl finds one under the tree on Christmas morning—and loves it. A child who receives this gift often saves it until he or she grows up and can enjoy it and share it with children and grandchildren. Have you guessed? Yep, it's a toy train set. Have you ever played with one?

Sometimes it's just a small set with the train choo-chooing around in a circle. Sometimes it can be set up in a room half-full of tracks, signal lights, toy trees, houses, churches, schools, and so forth for the train to travel around. It's fun to imagine you are riding ON the toy train, traveling far away from city to city. And it's most fun when you are riding around and around, sharing the fun with the best circles—friends and family.

Because there are not so many REAL trains today, collecting toy trains has become a popular hobby for kids and dads too. They often work on this fascinating hobby together.

Did you ever ride on a real train or collect toy trains or visit someone who has a train set up in his or her home or hear the song about the "Chattanooga Choo Choo"?

If you could take a real train ride, where would you like to go? As the train climbed slowly up a mountain, passed over a trestle, chugged along beside a river, or blew its whistle as it hurried through city streets—wherever you traveled—you would see many animals, vegetables, and minerals—all made by God.

Choo choo, fun, fun!

110

Does Your Computer Ever Have Bugs and Bytes?

Did you know that when the first computers were invented, they were made with vacuum tubes? Bugs (which can seem to get anywhere they want) liked to get inside those nice warm tubes, but when they did it often caused a short circuit. And that's when the computer inventors started saying their computer had a "bug." Did you know that?

Now those bugs didn't bite, but the computer people coined the word "byte" (short for "by eight") in 1959. It stands for a group of eight binary digits processed as a unit by the computer. If that sounds confusing, a lot of things about a computer are confusing, but what would we do without those bytes and system preferences and downloads and uploads and a "mouse" to run it all!

What do you like best about computers? Do you like to send e-mail to friends and maybe your grandma? Or do you know how to Twitter and text? Or would you rather send personal cards you make yourself or notes you write yourself?

It's always personal when you talk to God. He doesn't need a computer to get in touch with you—he sends birdsong and blossoms and blessings all the time. And you don't need a computer to get in touch with God—just a little prayer.

Extra! Extra!
Bonus Section Just For Fun

Do You Like to Ask Questions?

What kind of questions do you ask the most? Are they questions like this: Are we there yet? Do I HAVE to? Can we leave now? Why can't I? When will it be over? Please?

Do you ever ask questions like this: Who invented this? Why do people celebrate that every year? What's the name of this flower? When can we plant a garden? Where can we go to look for special rocks?

This book contains facts about inventions, celebrations, unusual flowers, good-tasting vegetables, and surprising kinds of rocks and jewels—but you might have MORE questions about them.

You can find answers to lots of questions in an encyclopedia or on the Internet. But don't ever stop asking questions. It's the only way to get smarter, to be surprised, and to make your life more fun!

Have You Ever Played Twenty Questions?

This is a game where somebody thinks of something, and then you have twenty questions to try to guess what that person is thinking.

The first question someone asks will usually be, "Is it animal, vegetable, or mineral?" Then you start asking questions about what size it is or where you would see it.

If you play that game you can find ideas in this book for things you can think about when you are "IT" and the questions you could ask when you are trying to guess. Here are some possible questions:

> Is it smaller than an iPod?
> Is it bigger than a watermelon?
> Is it like a heckelphone?
> Could you plant it in your backyard?
> Would you see it in a house?
> Would you see it in a church?
> Would you see it at a zoo?
> Could you eat it?
> Would you eat it?
> Can it fly?
> Is it alive?
> Is it soft or hard?
> Would it cost a lot of money?
> Is it made of wood?
> Would you want it for a pet?

Well, you get the idea, so you can think of your own questions.

Have fun!

Can You Tell Which Is Animal, Vegetable, or Mineral?

Here's a list of a variety of things you may have seen or heard about. Guess which one fits into which category. The answers are below.

1. Spaniel
2. Chalice
3. Kohlrabi
4. Magi
5. Monstrance
6. Poison ivy
7. Cassowary
8. Statue
9. Bulldog
10. Steeple
11. Dromedary
12. Pelican
13. Computer
14. Belfry
15. Asparagus
16. Pine tree
17. Garlic
18. Kerosene
19. Cassock
20. Cossack

ANSWERS

ANIMAL
1-4-7-9-11-12-20

VEGETABLE
3-6-15-16-17-19

MINERAL
2-5-8-10-13-14-18

138

Here Are a Few More Fun Facts to Share With Friends.

Choose the one you think is the funniest or your favorite.

* Humans have 639 muscles, but caterpillars have more than 4,000.
* A camel can drink up to 30 gallons of water at one time.
* A camel's hump stores fat, not water.
* The apple, the almond, and the peach are all members of the rose family.
* It is impossible to sneeze with your eyes open.
* Butterflies taste with their feet.
* There are 701 official breeds of dogs.
* Twenty percent of all road accidents in Sweden involve a moose.
* It is estimated that 6,800 languages are spoken by various people in various places in the world today.
* An elephant can smell water nearly 3 miles away.
* The most popular movie star in 1925 was a dog named Rin Tin Tin.
* The blue whale, the largest animal ever, weighs as much as 4 large dinosaurs, 23 elephants, 230 cows, or 1,800 humans.
* An onion can taste sweet if you eat it with your nose plugged.
* On average, 18 acres of pizza are eaten every day in the United States. (OK, pizzas are not made by God, but they ARE made with ingredients made by God—tomatoes, olive oil, peppers, onions, flour, mushrooms, and so forth.)

Try These Just for Fun

ANIMAL Car Card Game

Get some index cards OR pieces of construction paper the size of cards. Draw stick figures, or write the name of an animal on each card. (Remember, the Animal category includes birds, fish, bugs, and people.) Think of some you MIGHT see in your area instead of elephants or walruses. When you go on a car trip or if you go to a park for a picnic, see how many of these animals you can find. Whoever finds one first gets to keep the card. When the game is over, whoever has the most cards, wins.

(If you plan ahead and ask your mom to buy a box of animal crackers, that could be the prize. Or you could make a blue ribbon "award" of some kind.)

VEGETABLE Tie the Knot Rope Trick

Cut some two-foot (twenty-four inch) long pieces of string or rope. (Remember, the Vegetable category includes plants, and a piece of string or rope or twine can be made from cotton or the fiber of a plant called jute.) When some of your friends are together, give them each a piece of string, and tell them to hold it at each end and tie a knot in the string without letting go with either hand. THEN you show them the trick. Cross your arms so that your right hand is over your left elbow and your left hand is under your right elbow. Then pick up each end of the string with your hands in that position. When you uncross your hands, the string will automatically tie a knot!

MINERAL Penny Pitching Trick

For this game, you will need a penny, a tennis ball, and a friend. Put the penny on the sidewalk, then each of you take about ten paces back from it so that you are facing each other with the penny in the middle. Now bounce the tennis ball to your friend, trying to hit the penny on the way. If you hit the penny, you get a point. If the penny flips, you get two points. Then your friend takes a turn bouncing the tennis ball. The first one to get twenty-one points wins.

THREE-IN-ONE FUN

When you take a walk alone or with friends, look for round rocks like the shape of a head and smaller rocks like the shape of ears.

When you get home, glue the small MINERAL rocks on the round rocks to look like ears. Then use felt-tipped pens (made with VEGETABLE dyes) to paint on eyes, nose, and a mouth or teeth, and maybe whiskers to make an ANIMAL head paper weight.

More Questions to Find Some Answers

What is your favorite animal?

_____

Why is it your favorite animal?

_____

What is your favorite animal fun fact?

_____

What is your favorite vegetable?

_____

Why is it your favorite vegetable?

_____

What is your favorite vegetable fun fact?

_____

What is your favorite mineral?

_____

Why is it your favorite mineral?

_____

What is your favorite mineral fun fact?

_____

Write a story or draw
a picture about your
favorite animal,
vegetable, or mineral.

This Is the End—
but Not Really!

Although this book is ending, there is no end to the many fun facts you can discover that are God's creation. Keep looking, keep exploring, keep enjoying, and keep being grateful for so many facts and so much fun waiting to be found on and in the planet where you live!